Introduction

I have thought about writing this book for some time and as I approach my 30th year as a full-time professor, it seemed about right to do it now. For me, finding the appropriate title was very important, as it has always helped me with the development of manuscripts or other creative pursuits.

The title of this text emerged as I was taking a bus trip to visit a friend. During my visit, I decided that for my return trip I wanted to ride at the back of the bus, which at first glance, might seem fairly innocuous. However, since I am physically blind, I am considered by transportation personnel as an "ADA," which entitles me to ride on the front seat of the bus either just behind the driver or across from the driver. Knowing that many bus personnel would not even let me consider an alternative seating arrangement, I was prepared to fight that battle if necessary, to fulfill my desire for a backseat experience. Thankfully, the driver obliged, and I proceeded to the back seat of the bus for my return trip. The ride was fairly uneventful but I quickly discovered that riding on the backseat of the bus meant I was privy to a fairly constant parade of people using the bathroom. For me, from the backseat of the bus, the ride felt unusually noisy and it seemed that every bump, twist, and turn was heightened and amplified, but I appreciated having the opportunity to find this out firsthand.

As I sat there, the title of this book seemed to jump out at me. I am aware of the historical and rhetorical significance of the "back of the bus" metaphor and experience. I became astutely aware of the fact that I had the privilege of making such a choice and how relevant my choice might have been to the casual observer. With all of this in mind, I began thinking about my experiences as a blind and black professor and, in some ways, how my journey had metaphorically brought me from the back of the bus to the front of the classroom and what my experiences along the way might say to others in similar professional and personal life positions. I understand my unique position – I don't know many nor have I met many American-born, blind and black professors or those with Ph.D.'s – and the intersectionality of ableism and race is an intricate part of who I am and how others see me.

Occasionally, as an icebreaker, before some of my speaking presentations, I will ask my audience to close their eyes and then reopen them and tell me, as they look at me with my white cane, what do they see first? Is it my blindness, or my race, or a combination of both? The typical response to my query is that most of the audience sees me as a blind person first. It is my contention that they are inseparable and I will treat them as such throughout this text. The purpose here is to chart my experiences as a graduate student to thirty years of full-time teaching and researching in academia.

In chapter one, I thought it was important to talk about my graduate school experiences while pursuing the Ph.D. In chapter two, I explore the interview process and what it was like to obtain that first full-time position. In chapter three, I highlight how I got to Ohio University and why I remain here today; I also explore the pre-tenure and pre-promotion years. Chapter four explores the after-tenure and promotion years and the embracing of the 21st Century. Chapter five attempts to bring it all together with a discussion of relevant strategies and observations from a hindsight perspective. The memoir concludes with appendices, which includes a current vita, a sample publication, and a sample syllabus.

Chapter 1: Race and Ableism—My Graduate School Experiences

In August of 1985, I loaded most of my worldly possessions in the back of my grandparent's station wagon and left Gary, Indiana, heading for Detroit, Michigan. I was going to Wayne State University to pursue my Ph.D. in what was then called Speech Communication. Although I was born and raised in Chicago, Illinois, I had moved to Gary, Indiana in 1970. I packed a lot into the 15 years I spent in Indiana including a Bachelor's degree in History and Speech from Indiana University where I spent most of time on the Northwest Campus and a Master of Arts degree in Speech Communication from Purdue University (the Calumet campus).

I knew I wanted a PhD and I knew that Wayne State University was the place for me; partially because they were the only school that accepted me, albeit without funding initially, but more importantly, because that is where the woman who is now my wife wanted me to go. To this day, Regina has rarely steered me wrong. Equally adamant was my advisor at Purdue Calumet who had received his Ph.D. from Wayne State University and was sure it would be a good fit for me. I received my acceptance letter rather late in the admissions process, mainly because of procrastination on my part and others, so by the time I was accepted all the assistantships had been spoken for. If I wanted funding, it was incumbent upon me to plead my case directly to the Department Chair in hopes that some kind of funding might be found. I didn't just want funding, I needed it. So two weeks before the semester began, I sat in the office of the Department Chair and made my case. Thankfully, I was awarded a special fellowship that I have no doubt was specifically set aside for those from traditionally underrepresented populations. There's just something about the word "special" that makes it feel coded – as if the university were just waiting for the right candidate to check enough of the right boxes. Yet, it was the very fact that I checked those boxes by no choice of my own that I was able to pursue my dream. This initial experience really characterizes how my race and ability status have, for the most part, been positives for me. The fellowship paid for my tuition and, although I had to pay the taxes at the end of the year, it also included a generous monthly stipend. Although race and ability status are often framed as barriers to access, and they certainly can be, my early graduate school experiences made it abundantly clear that I also benefited because of my race and differently abled status.

My wife, Regina, and I were married in 1986 and looking back on those days I can't imagine going through that graduate school experience without her love and support. On top of a demanding full-time job, Regina was my full time cheerleader and provided as much support for my academic pursuits as was humanly possible. We enjoyed living in Detroit surrounded by the city's aggressive civil rights history and the welcoming environment for traditionally underrepresented populations. I particularly enjoyed the diversity of my classes in terms of race and ethnicity – likely a byproduct of Wayne State's open enrollment policy. This policy was not unique to Wayne State, but it was the first time I had experienced it and I relished what it did for the composition of my classes. It also seemed to change the campus. A week didn't go by where there wasn't some kind of racial or labor demonstration or protest happening on campus. So in those early days, it was really not my race that most concerned me, but my blindness. I find it telling that more than 30 years later my deepest memory relative to race in those early years is a seemingly benign conversation about hockey, but I also find it telling on an entirely different level that it has stuck with me for so long. I was having a random conversation about sports with a member of the faculty who was a well-known hockey fanatic. I forget now the specifics of the conversation, but the gist of it revolved around press conferences and athletes' rhetorical performances with reporters. The conversation ended with the faculty member boldly declaring, "Hockey players are the most intelligent, after all." I chuckled and mumbled something as I walked away, but then I thought about it later. In 1986, there were very few, if any, non-white hockey players and I wondered if he was trying to be funny or he really believed it. I must admit that because of my blindness, his nonverbals might have suggested that he was just trying to be funny, but as I think about it today, I think he was really serious. All these years later I want that conversation back so, if nothing else, I could respond to his comment.

Upon my arrival at Wayne State, I was given the same opportunity to teach given to all of the other teaching assistants and, also like all of the other teaching assistants, we taught public speaking. My reputation at Purdue as a blind teacher had proceeded me, so I was grateful to be trusted in the classroom. You're probably asking yourself right now, how does a totally blind person teach at all much less public speaking with its implicit emphasis on nonverbal communication. First, let me just say that I've witnessed my fair share of ill-equipped teachers who possess all five senses. Teaching like anything is a skill that must be honed based on one's capabilities. So I developed techniques and strategies that allowed me to be as effective as I could be in that context. I would position my chair as close to the speaking podium as possible so as to catch as many nonverbals, or the lack thereof, that I could. I had students in the class serve as peer evaluators to gain additional feedback and periodically

I would invite guests to provide official feedback on presentations as well. Most of my experiences as a teaching assistant are unremarkable; two, however, are indelible moments in my memory of these years.

The first took place amidst what started as a routine speech day. As the fourth speaker approached the podium the customary silence fell over the room. Then, seemingly out of nowhere, the blackboard exploded into what must have been a 100 little pieces. Immensely scared and unsure of what had just transpired, I remembered the Attention Getting Device on the student's outline simply stated, "I slam book on the floor to gain attention," but rather than dropping the book he threw it, literally, through the blackboard. After that class, I thought to myself, "who was blind?" I could only imagine what my face registered, but I think I can safely say that I was not the only one surprised that day. And then there was the time I was teaching a public speaking class as an adjunct at the University of Detroit. It was a cool, brisk, winter morning and I think we had about 7 speakers scheduled that day. A few days prior, one of the speakers had asked my permission to bring her pet to class to use during her demonstration speech. I said, "No problem" – I had so many of those kind of speeches before and so I thought nothing of it. I began to get concerned when she and her boyfriend placed a cage down beside me as she took her seat and waited her turn to speak. When it was her turn, she approached the podium where I had, as always, positioned myself immediately adjacent. My concern turned to fear as she neared the end of her introduction and motioned toward the cage and me. As she reached behind me into the cage to reveal her pet, Sam the Snake, and let it wrap itself around her just inches from my head, all I could think was, "Oh my." It was a good speech, I think, and the students seemed to enjoy it. I do remember one line quite clearly, though. She said, "He's very lethargic today because it's cold." Never have I been more thankful for the frigid Detroit winters than in that moment. She completed her speech, returned Sam back to his cage, and left the room with her boyfriend. That was the last time I ever saw Sam and also the last time I ever saw her. I can't be sure, but I hope it wasn't the look on my face that drove her from my classroom. Needless to say, I changed my demonstration policy after that. I would no longer allow live pets in the classroom and I continually warned people, "Please find effective, but safe, ways to gain the attention of your audience." My blindness radically changed the way I experienced these situations but I do not think it precipitated them.

Most of the time my blindness was a positive thing for me as a teaching assistant. It took some adjustment at first from everyone involved, but we would quickly catch our stride and by the end of the semester my blindness was a non-issue. Getting to that point with my own classes happened with an ease I did not fully recognize until I agreed to be a substitute instructor for one of my graduate student colleagues. He asked me to cover the class and to talk about developing the informative speech. I walked into the classroom, sat on the desk, and proceeded to be the "cool but relaxed" substitute. The desks in my colleague's class were set up in a semi-circle, so as the students took their seats I realized how close our proximity was but thought little of it. Everything was proceeding nicely, I thought, until about halfway through my lecture when a young lady, clearly frustrated, interrupted me. She pleaded, "Excuse me, could you take off your glasses, please? They are blinding me." I had forgotten to tell them I was blind and that my mirror shades weren't just an accessory to my cool substitute routine. Oops! Her frustration quickly gave way to embarrassment and now I was the frustrated one. I hadn't meant to make her feel uncomfortable, but I had taken for granted the easy rapport I built with my own students through early and honest conversations about my blindness. I still wear my fancy sunglasses and I think the cane I now regularly carry tends to give students a heads up, but ever since that day I have never started any class without addressing the issue of my blindness early on.

As you might expect, the issue of travel and mobility are quite significant when you are totally blind and although it gets easier when you have an established routine as a graduate student there is no such thing as a routine. Every semester meant finding my way to new buildings and spaces and determining the best way to move efficiently between them. Once I located my classroom for the semester, I surveyed the layout to determine how I could utilize the space to my advantage. These moments illuminated an even bigger issue I faced with my mobility – the need for independence. Although I appreciated the constant offers of assistance to help me navigate campus, I didn't want people to feel like they had to be responsible for me all the time. I thought to myself, "What is the best way for me to learn this campus as a blind man?" And I concluded, "Find another blind man on campus and learn from him!" Once again, fortune smiled on me, as I learned of a man who we'll call Jim working in the Disability Student Office. Jim and I instantly hit it off and grew to be great friends as he literally showed me as many aspects of that campus as he possibly could. My favorite lesson from Jim was what he lovingly called "The High Heels" method of travel. It was a sunny clear day and Jim and I were just starting out on our two-block journey from my building to one of our favorite restaurants. We were engaged in our typical banter when Jim suddenly brought the conversation to a screeching halt. "Listen," he said. "Listen to what," I inquired. We stood there silently as someone with loud clicking shoes, which Jim guessed to be high heels, scurried past us clearly in a hurry to get to their destination. Jim turned to me and gave me his instructions, our marching orders if you will. "Lock on to those steps and let's follow them." So we did – all the way to the restaurant. Looking back, I'm sure our behavior seemed odd to onlookers and I hope that this person didn't think we were stalking them, but they were providing a great source of information for us and because we could tune into their footsteps, we were able to move quickly to lunch. Technically Jim was no different from my colleagues who had offered to show me around campus – both were merely trying to help. But learning from Jim was different – perhaps because I wasn't necessarily learning from him, but alongside him. In our journeys together we both found a sense of independence.

I found Jim's "High Heel" mode of travel was particularly creative and effective especially since Jim had lost his sight fairly recently as a result of a work related accident in his 20's. I, on the other hand, have been blind basically since birth and I had never developed such a creative way to travel. My relationship with Jim was indicative of my positive relationship with the Office of Disability Services in general. I developed an effective working relationship with the staff and they helped me to find effective readers and scribes when necessary. One particular reader became indispensable to me. She was a retired accountant, who we'll call Elizabeth, that volunteered her time and, I dare say, she was an intricate part of my success in graduate school. We had long face-to-face reading sessions and Elizabeth read large amounts of material for me on tape. During my graduate school years, long before the advent of the internet or screen readers, I relied extensively on braille, a tape recorder, and live readers and scribes to keep up with my extensive workload. Over time, she became more of a colleague than just a reader given her deftness of reading quite complex material and her willingness to engage with me about the material when appropriate. Three decades later, I remain deeply grateful for the wonderful working relationship with that office during my graduate school days at Wayne State University.

As if traversing the 190-acre Wayne State campus weren't complicated enough, I also needed to learn the parts of Detroit that would be useful to me. Regina's schedule was scattered during our first years in the city; she would work 7-3 one day then 3-11 the next and even the midnight shift from time to time. Her hectic schedule kept us financially sound but also meant that I could not always depend on her to transport me back and forth between home and campus. In those early years, we lived about 30 minutes or no less than two bus rides from campus. Thankfully, I was a seasoned traveler with countless miles logged on busses, planes, and trains. I was also no stranger to long walks in unfamiliar territory. My white cane and I would strike out whenever it suited our fancy and most of the time we would eventually end up at our destination. Traveling for me wasn't just a necessity, it was a symbol of my independence and tangible proof to those around me that, with the proper training and attitude, a blind person could be an effective traveler. Naturally, there were times when I would catch rides with faculty and my graduate student colleagues when they were headed my way – I was self-reliant not stupid. I am grateful today for all those who gave me rides, especially on those nights when Regina worked late and our professors kept us in class until 9 or even 10 pm. Despite their perpetual kindness, I can still remember the sensation of standing alone in a bus shelter feeling the hands on my watch mark the time at 10 or 10:30 pm, hoping that the bus would come soon.

Traveling has always come easy to me; but that doesn't mean the travel itself was any easier than you might guess it would be for a blind person. Routines are a trade secret in the blind community bringing with them familiarity and normalcy, but more importantly efficiency and safety. During my time in Detroit, I rarely deviated from my routine. Before Regina and I married and moved into a place of our own, I rented a room from one of our church families. I knew every step of the one block journey from my front door to the bus stop and would have to be out of the house by 7:00 if I wanted to catch my bus to campus. As with any trusted routine, I never gave it much thought. I don't remember much about the morning that permanently altered this routine. That's the thing about routines though, they tend to rob of the little details. But on this particular morning as I approached my first corner, I heard a male voice call out, "I see you and you better keep going!" I ignored him but he continued to shout. "I will kill you!" I didn't know if he was talking to me or someone else or nobody else for that matter, but something told me not to look his way and certainly not to stop walking. I turned the corner with my back to him and headed for the main street where I usually caught my bus entirely unsure of what might happen next. Thankfully the man was all bluster and thankfully my bus was running on time that morning. Nevertheless, the experience really shook me up. I never left that early again. It was only a matter of time before those fearful feelings returned to me. I had gotten out of class early and rather than sticking to my routine which would entail a lengthy wait for my normal bus, I boarded the next bus headed to downtown Detroit where I would then transfer to my final bus home. It was the first time I had taken the bus downtown and I was enjoying the change of pace when about ten minutes into the ride a fight and a struggle broke out in the back of the bus. My heart raced and my head swirled with recent reports of shootings on busses across the city. Unable to truly size up the situation, I feared that this might be another one. The bus driver acted swiftly and was able to get police on the scene in a matter of minutes, but it became one more hazard and concern for me as a blind traveler. I always had to keep my wits about me; I always had to know who was around me and what was happening and to be aware of what it might take to maintain my safety. These moments didn't stop me from traveling but it did make me more aware of my needs as a traveler.

One more caveat about Jim and travel. By the way, he came to my wedding in 1986 and I sang at his in 1988. In the summer of 1988, Jim and I hatched a brilliant plan to embark on a marathon bus trip from Detroit to Wichita, Kansas to attend a church conference. At that time, a blind person could travel with the assistance of a sighted person on one ticket. So, Jim and I decided that he would pretend to be my sighted guide as we traveled across the country. It took us four busses and 28 hours to go from Detroit to Wichita, but we did it successfully. Well for the most part as I'm pretty sure there were times when the bus drivers knew that Jim didn't have very much sight either, especially when he would hit his head on the bus door or try to seat us in spots clearly occupied by other passengers. It was a hot August in Wichita and although I was really enjoying the conference there was something else I felt compelled to do on this trip. I wanted to explore the town and, if I could swing it, make my way to the Wichita State University and more specifically the Communication Department. With significantly less public transportation in Wichita than Detroit this journey was quite different than my previous adventures. Yet, I found the appropriate bus, eventually found both the University and the Communication Department, and I had a lot of fun doing it. I bring this up not to boast, but to reiterate that blindness does not have to hold one back from being creative and proactive. Jim and I made it safely back to Detroit and, ironically, on at least two of those bus rides we intentionally rode in the back on the bus. It was quiet and soothing and it gave us a sense of security and unexplainable comfort.

If you're anything like the countless graduate students I've advised over the years, you're undoubtedly curious about how I managed, logistically speaking, to complete my Ph.D. It certainly was not easy and I certainly wish I had access then to all the assistive technologies I have at my fingertips now, but it was manageable with an often frenzied combination of readers, recorded reading materials, and scribes. I was also fortunate to have been taught braille at an early age and by the time I arrived at Wayne State University as a proficient typist. Let me say, unequivocally, I cannot emphasize enough the importance of braille in the success of every aspect of my life. A word must also be said here, though, about scribes and the art of dictation. It is not easy to find or to trust someone to write for you and someone adept at taking dictation. This has never been clearer to me than when I began writing my dissertation. I vividly remember walking out of my advisor's office after a particularly intense meeting and wondering to myself, "I don't know if I can do this." Over the next two or three days I oscillated quickly between sheer panic and depression as I grappled with the enormous task of completing my dissertation. Ultimately, I literally ended up dictating most, if not all, of my dissertation to my wife. Night after night Regina would come home from her long shift at work and dutifully type every word I had prepared. I am tremendously grateful for her support and effort in that regard. One of the best decisions we ever made was to take $1,000 of our very meager funds and buy our first computer. It was the late 1980's so to call it a computer is probably an exaggeration; it was essentially a word processor, but it made all the difference to our efficiency. I can still remember the credit card we used and that $1,000 maxed it out!

The dissertation was the final but not the only hurdle to successfully completing my Ph.D. I, like countless graduate students before and after me, had to pass my comprehensive exams. Without the help of scribes and dictation this would not have been possible. At Wayne State University, graduate students were placed in a room and given four hours to compose a response to question created by the faculty members who had served as our instructors; we could either type our responses or write them by hand but had to complete them within the four hour time frame no matter which method we chose. Despite my proficiency with my braille typewriter, I knew that the four-hour time period necessitated something faster – well someone faster to be precise. Fully aware of the stress facing both me and them, I sought out two people one a dear friend and the other one of my graduate student colleagues who agreed to work as my scribes for those comprehensive exam responses. This unique arrangement warranted an equally unique space to complete the exams so we were placed in a room that allowed the grad director to see us at all times. If you're picturing an interrogation room you wouldn't be far off base. I can remember pacing the floor of the small room, furiously dictating to my scribes, and hoping they were getting it down right. Again, I am indebted to those very patient and professional people that wrote what I said and allowed me to be on equal footing with my peers.

Week after week, I would dictate paragraphs to my wife and before we knew it all 5 chapters and 100+ pages of the dissertation were complete. I will never forget the day my advisor said to me, "Okay, I think it's ready for the committee." In addition to the computer, we bought one of those inkjet printers and I can still hear the labored whirring sound it made as it struggled to print the requisite five copies of my dissertation—one for each member of the committee. I think it took about 10 hours and at least two ink cartridges to complete the task. On the day of the defense my wife and I showed up, along with most of the committee. I say most because my outside member (a black faculty member from History) decided the night before the defense that he would resign from the committee and not show up for the defense. You could only imagine my panic and dismay. To this day, I don't know what went into his decision, but once again, as fate would have it, the person assigned by the Dean to oversee my dissertation process was from History and he willingly stepped in to serve as my outside member. I have thought a lot about his choice to resign and I believe that, to put it bluntly, he did not feel that my dissertation was "pro-Black enough" or controversial enough. I say this because he had sheepishly made such comments in some of our previous meetings before the defense. I could be wrong, but nevertheless, the facts are what they are. My dissertation focused on the 1986 Michigan Gubernatorial Campaign, which pitted a black Republican conservative, William Lucas, against a white, moderate Democrat, James Blanchard. The race itself was controversial as most pundits had completely discounted Lucas as a viable candidate to win the Republican primary nomination. The campaign was filled with racial undertones and innuendos, and I did not want to contribute to that; so, instead, I took the high road with my study and used a Burkean Dramaturgical Approach to chart the successful campaign of James Blanchard and tried as much as I could to emphasize the positives of both candidates and their campaign strategies. Perhaps some people thought I should've taken the opportunity to be more racially invective, but that was not my personality nor did I think it was necessary. It was a historic campaign and, unfortunately, as much as Lucas tried to downplay his race and ethnicity, others sought to make it the essence of his being and campaign. I, too, could relate to this dilemma. Here are the actual title and words from the abstract of my dissertation:

A Dramatistic Analysis of Willian Lucas' 1986 Gubernatorial Campaign

This dissertation is a dramatistic analysis of William Lucas' bid to become America's first elected black governor. The study attempts to answer the question, why did Mr. Lucas, a consistently popular candidate in previous elections, fail so miserably in the 1986 gubernatorial race in Michigan?

The study employs Kenneth Burke's concept of dramatism as an overall method and Agenda Setting is used for imperical balance. In addition, Horatio Alger's concept of myth is used to show how the Lucas campaign tried to portray their candidate as Michigan's Alger hero.

The study concludes that Lucas' overall drama disintegrated into two opposing dramas, thereby, resulting in a double rejection from both black and white voters. The study further concludes that the rhetorical dilemma faced by William Lucas could have significant implications for black voters in the decade of the nineties.

I survived the defense by once again pacing around the room while talking

– which is when I do my best communicating in my opinion. I could not contain the tears when I was asked to come back into the room and was told that I had passed, especially since there had been some very traumatic defenses at that time in our department; I vividly remember one of my colleagues coming back to our graduate student office in tears after an unsuccessful defense. I had survived. All of it.

All the reading, dictating, and trying to find creative ways to be successful in my classes and all the other aspects of my program had finally paid off. My dream had become a reality. It was a dream that started in an undergraduate communication course at Indiana University in 1979. After changing my major four times within the first two years of college, it was in that class that I finally decided I wanted to be a communication professor, much like the wonderful woman that was teaching that class on that day. Nine years later, because of a lot of hard work, a great support system including family, friends, and most importantly, my wife, I could now officially call myself Dr. Smith. I think I can honestly say that, for the most part, my race and ethnicity and my differently abled status had been more positive attributes for me rather than negative. I will say more about this in my final chapter, but I believe that there were times when my blindness counteracted my blackness and my blackness positively influenced my blindness.

When it came time for my exit interview with the graduate director I was left with the lingering question facing most, if not all, graduate students: "Will I ever get a job?" After some minor chit-chat, I mustered up the courage and bluntly asked the Director, "What do you think are my chances of getting a job?" And I shall never forget his response. He said, "You are Black, you are blind, and you are a male. I have no doubt that you will get a job." What a statement, and I believe that he meant it and believed it himself. It was not long before I had at least three job offers and had to make decisions about that next chapter in my life.

Chapter 2: Getting That First Job

It was the fall of 1988 when I received a call from one of my peers that because of a foreseeable maternity leave, she would not be able to complete her spring semester at her present university. I could tell she wasn't just calling to tell me the good news and I was right. After offering her my congratulations, she made the real reason for her call clear to me. "Would you be interested in taking my full-time position in spring semester, with the possibility of applying for a tenure track job here," she asked. I wanted to be surprised that she had called me with such an opportunity, but it felt more like fate. You see, this wasn't the first time a fortuitous offer from her turned into something great; in fact, my dissertation topic had come as a result of a report she did on that 1986 Michigan Gubernatorial Campaign in one of our classes. She said to me, "Why don't you take all of my data because I don't plan on doing anything else with it, and this could be great dissertation topic for you?" Boy, was she right. I talked it over with my wife and we concluded that it was something we should consider and we were soon on our way to Southbend, Indiana to see what might be possible. The interview was successful and I was offered the position on the spot, but I was told in my letter of acceptance to mention that

I would be interested in being a candidate for the full-time, tenure track position as well. So it was back to Indiana for Regina and I!

Still unsure of whether my new position at Indiana University, Southbend would turn into a permanent gig, I continued preparing for the other interviews I already had lined up. I was fascinated with how the interviewers approached me and how they chose to deal with my race and ethnicity and blindness. Sadly, many were uncomfortable and were not just awkward, but often demonstrated ineptness and ignorance. They had to tread lightly, however, as to them I represented a promising candidate to check the requisite diversity box and meet a quota. Throughout this process, I couldn't help feeling that they wanted me for all the wrong reasons. I repeatedly encountered interviewers that could not use the word blind or did not know how to interact with someone like me. I remember one job interview where the Dean wanted to have lunch with me after our meeting, but for the life of him, he couldn't figure out how the hell he was going to get me over to the cafeteria. I just wanted to scream at him and say, "Let's just stand up, turn around, and walk out the door for a start?" Then, at lunch, he literally chose to speak to everyone else in the pompously named Executive Room except for me. Needless to say, when I received a job offer from that university, I declined. I have always tried to abide by the philosophy that the best time to interview for a job is when you have one. Fortunately, this has mostly been true for me. So, when I encountered interviewers incapable of interacting with me and clearly interested only in my minority status, I relished the chance to play head games and sarcastically toy with them, knowing that there was no way we would become colleagues.

In January 1989, I sat in my office at Indiana University, Southbend (IUSB) and prepped for my first class as a full-time visiting professor in Speech Communication. As I walked towards the classroom, carefully following the route I had charted days earlier, my mind raced with equal parts anticipation and exhilaration, but ambivalence and nervousness as well. I had a total of four classes that semester, but this being the first made it feel all the more stressful. I walked into the room where my 25 or so students sat waiting for me. I introduced myself as Dr. Smith and explained, "I can't see you physically because I am blind, so that means that raising your hand will probably not get my attention." This would become my opening line for most of my classes for the next 30 years - always met with small laughs and awkward silence in equal measure. I remember coming home that day to the house we rented on campus and telling my wife, "One day down, and who knows how many to go!" It was a small campus, so getting around was not at all difficult – especially given the close proximity of our home. Even though I had spent 15 years of my life in Indiana, I did not know much about Southbend other than Notre Dame, of course. It was a small department, the kind where people stick around for their entire career, composed of just two or three full time faculty and a handful of adjuncts. In fact, the vacancy I was hoping to fill had only become available after a faculty member of more than 25 years decided to retire. Later that spring, I interviewed for the job and was extended an invitation to join the faculty permanently. In just a matter of months, I had gone from Visiting Professor to a senior member of the Communication Department.

As you might expect, my job at IUSB involved teaching a variety of public speaking courses including both introductory and upper level classes. Although I never encountered any more snakes, there are a few events from those years that linger in my memory. The first occurred when I had a student that was legally blind or what we in the blind community consider just enough sight to be dangerous to themselves and others in the right situation. They also were committed to pretending to see more than they could and to hiding their blindness. This wasn't like Jim pretending to see to get a free ticket on the Greyhound, this was more about refusing to come to terms with their condition. As this was an upper level course the emphasis was on more advanced presentations and modes of delivery with the expectation that they would have mastered several key skills in the introductory course. During their first speech, I noticed that this student spoke in a very robotic manner more characteristic of an elocutionary style than the extemporaneous style required by the assignment. I mentioned this in my written comments to this student and they informed me that they were doing the speech from memory and that their outline was just a prop. It was then that I found out that they were legally blind and had chosen to do a lot of things from memory. Knowing how difficult it can be to master a memorized speech, I warned the student that foregoing the outline is a risk because it wouldn't take much for you to forget. "Oh, no!" they informed me, "I've got it down to an art." I said, "Okay, but remember, that's why we use the outline and notecards because that is the essence of extemporaneous speaking." Needless to say, about halfway through their second speech, my concern became reality as a member of the audience began furiously coughing and sneezing making it impossible for him to remember what came next. My heart sank as he struggled to complete the speech. Hoping that this would be a wakeup call, I once again pleaded with them, "You need to find ways to compensate for your lack of vision and you need to stop denying your blindness." Unfortunately, I don't think this student ever came to terms with their blindness, but at least it wasn't for my lack of trying.

Low moments like the one I mentioned previously where thankfully few and far between and for the most part my students at IUSB consistently challenged both themselves and me to be better. In the fall of 1989, one of my students was wheelchair bound after being paralyzed and subsequently had very limited vocal strength and clarity. Despite these challenges, the student was quite successful in my class because collectively we chose to give them every opportunity to succeed. As an audience we had to listen very closely and we had to compensate for their lack of podium presence and non-verbal options, but we all made it work. At its core, public speaking is as much about the audience making the speaker feel comfortable and so that is what we, as a class, did for them as best we could. Then, there were my rappers. Yes, I said rappers. I was a bit perplexed when two students came to me one day and told me that, as far as this public speaking thing was concerned, they didn't really get it. In their words, they were just brothers "from the hood" who could never be comfortable speaking like everyone else. When I asked them how they expected to pass the class they bluntly told me, "We don't know." Refusing to let them accept defeat so quickly I said to them, "What do you like to do?" They told me that they liked hip-hop and writing their own raps. So, admittedly unsure of how it would turn out, I said to them, "Then rap all your speeches." I must tell you that I wish to this day that I had video recorded some of their presentations. From their speeches of introduction to their persuasion speeches, they delivered the most profound and effective raps I have ever heard. Their impressive raps made them notorious in our class and even around campus as several students invited their friends to attend class when these two young men were scheduled to speak. That first year involved a lot of teaching, a lot of parenting, and a lot of adjusting to a new world.

There was one eerie development during a section of public speaking that still resonates with me. One of my black, female students gave her speech about her brother, who had recently passed away due to the early onset of cancer. As she spoke, I felt very strongly that this was a significant experience that demanded my full attention. When she mentioned her brother's name, I almost jumped out of my chair. You see, her brother had been a star basketball player on the Southbend High School team in 1972. I used to listen to those games on the radio in Gary, Indiana, and I remember following the exploits of that team very closely. I felt as if I knew the team's two-star players, one of which was her brother and the other of which was the current and present basketball team's coach of the high school located across the street from my house. Even though that team lost the state championship game that year, a part of me always felt like I wanted to meet her brother. I never got to meet him, but here she was in my class, talking about him 20 years later.

I enjoyed my life in Southbend. Eventually, we would buy a house about two blocks from my office and it was so wonderful to be able to get up and walk those two blocks to my office at any time of the day or night that I chose to. The move came just in time for the birth of our first child. In January 1990, after 18 hours of labor and an eventual C-section, Ebony was born. I can still remember them putting my daughter in my arms and how scared to death I was that I might drop her. I remember bringing her home in a cab stuffed to the brim with balloons, and thinking to myself, "I have a new job and a new child. Let the fun begin." My wife was a real trooper at this time, holding down the fort, raising our daughter, and generally keeping me in line most of the time. I remember one day she called me at the office and she said, "I hear strange noises in the basement." With a full class schedule that day, I had no time to run home so I asked one of my new colleagues at the university to go to our house and check on her. Upon closer inspection, they discovered a bird had somehow crawled in through an old coal shaft in the back of the house and gotten lost in the basement. Obviously panicked, the bird was furiously flying toward the window trying to get out. My wife said that my colleague wanted no part of the bird and he was just as afraid as I might've been if I had come home! So much for the sighted-guy to the rescue, right? We called the Animal Control Office and they came and got the bird out. This incident sits with me not because of its apt depiction of first-time homeowners, but because it illuminates how easy it is for people to hold such erroneous notions about the limitations of someone who is blind. I would have tried to handle the bird as best I could have, but because my sighted colleague assumed otherwise I was never even given the benefit of the doubt.

One highlight for me while serving in that first job at IUSB was joining an organization that I had known about for some years, but, for a number of reasons, had chosen not to be a part of. In 1990, a reporter from the Southbend Tribune decided that it was time to do one of those nice stories about the new blind professor in town. It was your typical story, which characterized me as this amazing blind person that could probably even walk up and down stairs and get a drink of water at the fountain without assistance. Even though I repeatedly tried to redirect the reporter and de-emphasize those kind of foci that was the eventual perspective of the piece. I remain thankful for the story not for its lack luster content, but for bringing me to the attention of several other blind people in the community who subsequently invited me to a local chapter meeting of the National Federation of the Blind of Indiana (NFB). Several of my friends from high school were long time members, but they had never actively sought to recruit me. This was probably a good idea at the time because even though I had heard of the NFB, and sometimes read their literature, I really had no interest in joining the organization while I was in college. I soon joined their chapter as well as the Indiana state affiliate because it seemed right and timely and was eager to become involved in the organization. I remember taking a nap early in 1992 at my home in Southbend when I was awoken by the loud ring of the telephone. The voice on the phone greeted me and politely said, "Are you Dr. John Smith? And if you are, Dr. Jernigan would like to speak with you." That call took my breath away. If you're not familiar with Dr. Kenneth Jernigan the best way to describe him is essentially as the Martin Luther King Jr. of the blind community. So the fact that he was calling me was unbelievable. I sat in shock on the other end of the line as he invited me to attend the 1992 NFB National Convention in Charlotte, North Carolina and offered me the necessary financial support to attend. To this day, I am a member of the NFB and will be for the rest of my life essentially because of that call. Whenever I think about my first job in Southbend, it will include my introduction to the NFB, as they are inextricably linked. When I attended that first national convention in 1992, I discovered that there were other blind educators, and blind people in general, living their lives and making a difference, as I was trying to do. After years of navigating my professional life, often feeling alone on the journey, I felt as if I had found an extended family. I can say honestly and without hesitation that finding the NFB made me a better professor and person in every respect.

Awkward job interviews aside, my dual status of blackness and blindness continued to be positive experiences for me in my early professional years. I would routinely get calls from former professors and administrators about coming back to Indiana University and Purdue. Once again, I must hasten to add, while I believe those efforts were sincere I also think they were guided by the increased need for diversity on their campuses and in their faculty. In 1991, the institution where I completed my Bachelor's degree, Indiana University, Northwest, gave me the honor of serving as their honored speaker on MLK Day; during that visit, once again, I was approached about "coming home." I was invited back to Purdue Calumet to speak to the graduate students in an informal effort to re-recruit me once again. These attempts were both flattering and, I believe, genuine. However, I was quite comfortable in Southbend and I was committed to literally building a new department from scratch. I say from scratch because, in my second year there, the Dean of our college invited me to breakfast and I could tell by his tone that he wanted to have one of "those talks." Between wonderful bites of bacon and eggs and Bob Evans biscuits, he informed me that the administration was considering creating a brand-new College of the Arts program with house music, theater, fine arts, and maybe speech. The maybe being contingent on me and my willingness to leave my current home in the Arts and Sciences College aligned with English and a handful of other subjects and join the new arts focused program. As I sat there, I thought about the phrase, "Follow the money!" It was clear to me that the administration was prepared to sink a lot of money into this new endeavor, and a part of me believed that this would ultimately be a boon for our program. I thought back to my brief meeting months prior with the chair of the music department, who I might add had quite a reputation as being a very vocal and flamboyant administrator and individual. He would be the first Dean of this new program and, quite honestly, we hit it off from the beginning. I think it helped that I was a musician and performer as well (I often say I teach by day and sing by night). I found him to be a straightforward and "what you see is what you get" kind of fellow. He was the kind of person I wanted to work with and so just like that I jumped head first into the burgeoning College of the Arts at IUSB.

This new arrangement and relationship ushered in what I will call "the view from the other side of the table." Despite my status as a so-called junior faculty member, I was now the most senior and experienced faculty member in our new department. It was up to me to build a new team and this time I would be the one doing the hiring and firing; I was now the interviewer. One of my first tasks was to hire a black graduate student from my alma matar, Purdue Calumet. To be clear, we did not hire him because he was black, but because he clearly was the most qualified. However, it did help to have someone like him in an office right next door to mine. Eventually, he and I would attend Communication conferences at the regional and national level in an effort to recruit others to join us. As I sat there in my official capacity greeting candidates I fought back the urge to pinch myself just to make sure that this was real. It was an exhilarating time and position for me as a young faculty member and I must tell you that things looked pretty different at those conferences from this particular side of the table. A few years later, I had the honor of helping our new hire with his application to the Ph.D. program at Wayne State University. He was successful and it was a bittersweet day when he left our department at IUSB and went to Detroit to pursue his Ph.D. In my mind, this was the ultimate "pay it forward."

In my new capacity as senior faculty member of our Communication Department, I could select pretty much any class I wanted to teach and as a regional campus of Indiana University, we could offer any class on the books. One day, while looking over the potential class offerings, I discovered a course entitled, "Communication in Black America." It intrigued me and I ultimately decided to offer it in 1992. I only got to teach it one time at IUSB, but it provided some of my most profound experiences in the classroom. I remember I ended up with about 13 students for the class and about nine of them were Black Americans. It was the first time I had ever taught a class where Black Americans were the dominant audience. I had prepared what I called an "ABC" syllabus because I thought that my audience would be predominantly Caucasian and Euro-American and that, at most, we could only cover the basics. About halfway through the course, I discovered that we needed a "XYZ" syllabus. It was particularly enlightening to see how my Euro-American students reacted to being in the minority, especially given the topic of the course. Unfortunately, most of them did not react well and never quite found their comfort zone. To this day, I wonder if they really understood the significance of that learning experience – the classroom dynamic was in and of itself a lesson for the keen observer. My black students routinely spoke out, spoke back, and conversed loudly, even during my lecture format (call and response), when something particularly impacted and enthralled them. My Euro-American students thought this was rude and disrespectful. Not only would they tell me that I should, "Do something about it," they frequently made their feelings known to the black students as well accompanied I'm sure by some very stern nonverbals. It was then that I was able to talk about the power of the spoken word in the Black community and the significance of call and response in achieving balance and harmony in small group communication in the culture. At least one other annoying development in that class caused great consternation. Several of my black students would routinely come to class late and, when they came to class late, they would make sometimes the most flamboyant and outrageous arrivals and entrances. There were no apologies, for the most part, and they basically implied the class doesn't get started really until they arrived. I must admit that I had been trained by Euro-Americans to teach predominantly other Euro-Americans and this arriving late upset me at first as well. And then it hit me. This is the time to talk about those unique cultural exigencies relative to the Black culture, one of those being the use of time. I was able to show the class that in large segments of Black America, time is not viewed as a commodity, but as a present happening. It was called "CP time," or "Colored Peoples' time." That is to say, things start when I get there and they go as long as they need to. I was able to share with my Euro-American students that in many Black churches, it is common for services to last five or six hours and even longer. I was also able to tell them that if someone invites you to a party or event that they say will start at 8pm, I would not necessarily show up until 9 or 10pm if the audience will be predominantly Black. What fascinating teaching moments came from that course and, as you will see later in my story, they will become recurrent themes in another class that I would offer at another university.

For the most part, my race and ethnicity was not controversial or brought a lot of attention to me in that first job. However, it became clear that many of my ideas and philosophical assumptions tended to be more conservative than most of my non-White colleagues. In 1993, I felt the need to publish some comments regarding the annual MLK Day activities in the community. If there had been doubts as to my political and philosophical mindset and allegiance, this "in your face" article published in the local newspaper dispelled them.

OPINION □ South Bend Tribune □ Monday, January 18, 1993 □ A9

Many African-Americans are losing sight of King's dream

By JOHN W. SMITH

Today marks the official observation of the 64th birthday of Rev. Martin Luther King Jr. It is a time for all African-Americans to pause and reflect on the state of "the dream."

My reflection on the state of "the dream," 25 years after King's assassination, is filled with sadness and frustration. The fact is, many African-Americans have forgotten the true meaning and essence of "the dream." I have often heard African-American leaders and politicians equate "the dream" with more welfare, housing projects, abortion rights and any other handouts to which they feel African-Americans are entitled. This was not King's true vision.

For those who doubt this, a simple reading of Lerone Bennett's "What Manner of Man" and a re-read of King's "Birmingham Jail Letters" would set the record straight. The essence of "the dream" was not about what the white man owed to blacks. It was all about equality.

King was not a beggar. He carried himself and taught his people to carry themselves in such a way

MICHIANA POINT OF VIEW

as to earn respect and equality. He talked about African-Americans "standing up and straightening their backs so that whites could ride them as long er." He challenged African-Americans to be the best at what they could, be it a street sweeper or an astronaut. When African-Americans limit themselves to a request for more welfare and not job training, African-Americans are not standing up straight and proud, but rather are bending over to carry the racism of the elite.

In his famous "I Have A Dream" speech, King wanted blacks to be "judged by the content of their character and not the color of their skin." When African-Americans demand quotas and special programs most often they are not being judged by their abilities but by their color. When they allow the American Civil Liberties Union, the National Association for the Advancement of Colored People, the Congressional Black Caucus and the Rainbow Coalition to demand that they be given fish rather than

being taught how to fish, they are not fighting for civil rights but rather for special favors.

The time has come for African-Americans to take control of their own destiny and stop looking to and blaming all of the ills of their communities on white people. Blacks must demand that their people learn the American economic system, are better educated at the middle and high school levels and understand that anyone can achieve a full education with loans, financial aid and hard work.

The idea that African-Americans need handouts to survive has caused them to raise a generation of people who are angry because they think that white America owes them something. I don't want my 5-year-old daughter to grow up with this mentality. African-Americans must teach their children that they are somebody not only because of what they can get out of the government but because of what they are willing to contribute toward their own success in life. History records African-Americans as a strong people. The struggles through slavery, Jim Crow and

the civil rights movement are indicative of black people's ability to persevere.

This ability to survive may be severely threatened by the ravages of alcohol, drugs, abortions, AIDS and gang warfare which, unfortunately, have become the norm in many communities. If blacks are to continue to survive as a people in this country, we must look within ourselves and our communities for the solutions to these social problems.

Reflect on King's "dream" and be angry because while many of our leaders made it to the promised land via special privileges, quotas and the like, an entire generation of black people are forever trapped in the twilight zone of poverty and disrespect. Our leaders must come to a true understanding of what "the dream" is all about, and this understanding must begin with us. "The dream" was and is still about equality, opportunity and respect.

John W. Smith, a South Bend resident, is an assistant professor of speech communications at Indiana University South Bend.

My time at IUSB was magical and fulfilling. Once again it seemed that my race and ethnicity and differently abled status were positive attributes for me. I was asked to serve as the Campus Parliamentarian for the entire faculty senate. I was asked to serve on the very prestigious committee that was charged with reviewing the Chancellor and deciding whether to recommend re-appointment. Although this was a particularly intense assignment as the then Chancellor was quite a character, the fact that I was entrusted to serve on this committee was indicative of my rising visibility and impact at IUSB. In 1992, the campus held a big presidential election forum. It was a memorable campaign because of the candidacy of Ross Perot. Again, I was chosen to speak and to offer expert comments about how the various campaigns were proceeding and what the final outcome might be. It is fair to say that this was an ideal first job for me. Thanks to the significant tuition waiver granted to faculty members, Regina was able to go back to school and finish her Bachelor's degree. My daughter, Ebony, was able to attend the excellent daycare on campus and I would routinely finish my classes in the afternoon, swing by and pick her up, and literally carry her the two blocks home so that we could watch Mr.

Rogers together. As a blind professor, all the stars aligned. I could walk to my office at any time and back home, I could pick up my daughter at any time, and I was a part of the most visible and financially successful collaboration on campus. Never in my wildest dreams could I have imagined leaving this environment in the manner in which I did. As wonderful as things were, sometimes life beckons to us in the strangest ways. We can decide either to heed the call or ignore it. That call came for me literally out of the blue and it would change my life forever.

Chapter 3: The Pre-Tenure Years—How I Got to Ohio and Why I Stayed

My time in Southbend coincided with several "firsts" in my life. It was the birthplace of my first child and it was where we bought our first house. It was where I had my first full time teaching position and administrative experience. It was also where I received my first real computer and, I must tell you, I was not impressed. To be honest, there was a part of me at that time that believed that I would never ever really use the thing. I begrudgingly learned to use it and discovered its true potential after sending my first email message and receiving an almost instantaneous reply. Not only was I hooked, but I soon realized just how significant this machine would be both for me and for our society. Technology promised to truly level the playing field, especially for the differently abled community, but I will save those thoughts for a later chapter. I was quite content with all aspects of my life in Southbend, Indiana with no intentions of leaving and certainly not to rural Ohio. I was born and raised in Chicago, spent my teenage and early adult years in Gary, Indiana, and went to graduate school in Michigan. I had spent my entire life in the states surrounding Ohio, but never thought I would find myself living there.

Ironically, I had spent part of the 80's and 90's performing at clubs, churches, and other musical venues in Ohio. If I had known what the future held for me, I might've taken some notes during some of those gigs. So how did I get to Ohio? And why am I still here? Here is the story.

It started in November of 1991 when I attended the National Communication Association (NCA) conference along with one of our newly hired colleagues to recruit a new faculty member for our growing department. As the event drew to a close and we made our way out of the venue, my colleague browsed the table at the front of the room now home to a collection of discarded job advertisements. He picked one up and began reading. I thought he was simply sizing up our competition when he turned to me and said, "This sounds like a job for you!" I pretended not to hear him and he, more forcefully this time, repeated himself. I retorted, "I have a job and it's all good." When he brought up the advertisement again several hours later, I thought I should at least hear the language of the advertisement. As he read it to me, I grew more confident in my rejection. "Are you crazy? This is not for me." The position was for an Assistant Professor in The School of Interpersonal Communication at Ohio University in Athens, Ohio. I had never heard of the school, much less the town, and my area was Rhetoric and Public Address, not Interpersonal Communication. I thought my emphatic response to his reading of the advertisement would finally put things to rest. However, on the plane back to Southbend, he said, "I think you ought to apply for that job." For at least two weeks thereafter he would repeatedly pop into my office and prod me about my application status. So to shut him up – and for the record I do not recommend this as a reasonable response to such annoyances – I threw together a letter of interest. As I passed his office on the way to the mailbox I said, "Please stop bugging me about this job. I'm going to apply just for the hell of it!" I totally forgot about the whole ordeal until about a week later when

I received a phone call from the Director of Ohio University's School of Interpersonal Communication (INCO). I sat silent and slightly confused as she discussed the position with me and invited me to campus for a formal interview. I fought the urge to interrupt her, "Lady, please forgive me. I was just joking and I sent you that letter just to shut up my colleague." I waited for my opportunity to decline politely, but was completely caught off guard when she inquired as to where she should send my plane ticket and where I wanted to fly into. I felt so bad, and so naïve, thinking to myself "Oh my God. They've spent their hard-earned money because of me on a stupid joke." My conscience got the better of me and I decided to go on the interview. After all, what harm could it do?

Just because my initial application was a joke didn't mean I wouldn't do my due diligence to prepare for the interview. As I began my investigation of the department and the university, two things seemed to strengthen my argument that this was not the place for me. First, although the school did have a rhetoric component, consensus across the discipline at this time was that if you were a rhetorical scholar then this was not the place for you. Second, I discovered that, because of a number of factors, it was the belief in the Ohio differently abled community that Ohio University was not a good place for the differently abled. You're probably thinking this was the end of the story, right? And of course, you would be wrong. I soon received my ticket and my itinerary; I would be flying into Columbus, Ohio and staying for about four days. When I arrived in Columbus, Ohio, a very kind and conscientious faculty member picked me up and we headed for Athens. When I said we headed for Athens, I mean we drove, and drove, and drove! We stopped for dinner in a small town named Lancaster, Ohio and then we kept on driving. All I could think was "Where is this place?" I knew the town was rural, but I didn't realize it would be quite the trek. Upon arriving at the hotel at about nine or ten that night, and after the departure of my wonderful host, I turned on the television.

Only two stations came through and one of them was exclusively covering the City Council meetings. Hoping for something better, I turned on the radio, only to discover a meager three stations all of which were playing Country Western music. My apologies if you're a fan of Country Western music, but in my opinion it is an acquired taste that I simply do not have. I sat down on the bed and I said to myself, "What have I done and where am I?" As I looked back over my itinerary all I could think was "What are we going to do for four days down here?"

It was on the third day that I called my wife and said what many husbands have said and will probably continue to say from time to time, "I think we have a problem." She said to me, "What is our problem?" I sheepishly retorted, "I think I like it!" "You can't like it," she exclaimed! Still baffled by my own revelation I said, "I know, and believe me, I've done everything I could to sabotage this trip." It was true. I intended to be a real jerk and to play head games throughout the trip, as I had in previous interviews. Despite my best effort all my defenses were overcome and for the first time in my short faculty life, I had found a department that I really believed wanted me for all the right reasons. To them, I was not just a blind professor, but a professor that just happened to be physically blind. The first thing I noticed was how comfortable the faculty was with me and how willing they were to ask me real and difficult questions about how I did my job and how I would continue to perform as a member of this faculty. They were not afraid to use the word "blind" and there were at least two other Black faculty and at least three other People of Color represented on the faculty. The other faculty members seemed genuinely comfortable with my race and ethnicity and treated me with amazing respect and genuine graciousness. I believe that you can find out a lot about people during social activities like meals and informal gatherings so I paid careful attention to the behavior of my potential future colleagues during these events. It's during these moments when people put their guard down that you truly get a sense of how they feel towards you. I remember during my teaching demonstration the enthusiastic and genuine support I received from the faculty and even the graduate students in attendance. At the risk of being very stereotypical, on the second day of my trip I mentioned to somebody that I really liked fried chicken and one graduate student eagerly volunteered to take me to a place I now frequent regularly – Miller's Chicken. Good food is a powerful thing and after a visit to Miller's Chicken, I was beginning to reconsider my blunt rejection of Athens. It was some of the best chicken I had in a long time, and I have eaten fried chicken from one end of this country to the other! I would later say to someone, "They've got to have somebody Black tied up in the kitchen cooking that chicken!" As I sat in the office of the Director of the School before my departure, I was stunned at the possibility of leaving Southbend and coming to the foothills of Appalachia. I would later learn that Ohio University had a very aggressive Affirmative Action policy and process and that they were willing to spend the money to fulfill their mission statement. I limped home in a fog and positive stupor and waited for a possible offer – still unsure of whether or not I was ready for such a huge and unexpected change. The offer came a few days later and we had to make some tough decisions. It had all happened so fast; I half-heartedly applied in December and was surprisingly offered the job in early February of 1992. After discussing it with my wife, I decided to push the envelope one more time. I told the Dean of the College that I would make the move only if, by chance, they would hold my position for a year to let me effectively wrap up things in Southbend. I knew that this would be a deal breaker and then I could get on with my life. The Dean said to me, "No problem. See you next year!" These people were full of surprises.

With this year in hand, I had a chance to have a long farewell and separation from Southbend and get things settled at IUSB. We made several trips to Athens to look for a house and in 1993, we put our home on the market in

Southbend – it sold in just a week! In August of 1993, we headed to Athens, Ohio with our three-year-old daughter and my wife's undergraduate degree in hand. We arrived on a hot, humid day and were fortunate to snag another great house that was formerly owned by the founder of the school. We've always had remarkable luck with housing and, much like our previous home, our new house in Athens had only been lived in by one other family. They wanted to "keep it in the family" and thankfully saw us as an extension of their family given my new position at the university. So that's how we got to Ohio, but why we yet remain is the rest of the story.

My first decade at Ohio University was truly amazing. My first impressions of the faculty had not betrayed me –the faculty was racially and culturally diverse and the Director was genuinely concerned with making everybody feel comfortable and productive. I was surprised, however, to learn how rewarding it was and would become for me to work with Ph.D. students – I hadn't had the chance to do this in a formal capacity at IUSB and couldn't grasp the significance of these experiences until I had them for myself. In my first year in the School of Interpersonal Communication, I was asked to co-direct the dissertation of a Black female graduate student. Since then I have directed or served on the dissertation committee of at least eight Black American students. There were several such opportunities with international students as well. I bring this up because one might think that given the geographical and cultural location of Athens, Ohio, that we would not have such a wealth of diversity amongst our doctoral students. It was amazing to witness these Black Americans fulfill their dreams and transform into productive scholars in all aspects of our discipline, both regionally and nationally. I don't know if, during that time, other programs had this kind of success when it comes to traditionally underrepresented populations, but I must honestly tell you it reaffirmed my belief that my decision to leave Southbend was indeed the right one.

It was wonderful to have other Black colleagues in our school and, after a bit, I discovered that there were a number of Black faculty scattered throughout the university as well. One in particular, a faculty member in the Philosophy Department, gently took me under their wings and through genuine mentorship strove to make me feel even more comfortable in my new world. He would become not only my neighbor, but a genuine friend. We served together on several dissertation committees and one experience I shall never forget really strengthened our bond. In 1995, the university was interested in having a healthy dialogue about the pros and cons of Affirmative Action and facilitated a series of public debates on the topic to increase connections and interactions with alumni around the state. My colleague and I agreed to a take the stage on opposing sides and would soon travel to cities across the state to duke it out including Cleveland and Cincinnati. The debates were quite popular and on one occasion we held five or six of these forums over a two-day span. It was a fun, healthy, and intellectually stimulating experience and even though we were on opposite sides of the issue we treated each other with courtesy and respect. We hoped to show the audience the potential of peaceful deliberation and I hope they left the debate feeling as satisfied as we did. Experiences like this help me connect with other Black faculty on campus and the intellectual and social interactions were not just stimulating, but became an intricate part of my faculty participation at the university.

Junior faculty are frequently the target of unsolicited advice from those who've already climbed the academic ladder, and although I took most of it with a grain of salt there was one suggestion I quickly adopted: Act like you're tenured even before you get tenure and you won't have to worry about it. So, that is what I did. Thankfully, I was part of a faculty that never made me feel like my opinion did not matter. In fact, it was not just welcomed but, I felt, valued and encouraged. I was not just relegated to the "race and differently-abled" stuff, but was given choices about committee assignments and how much I wanted to work at every level of the school. I quickly developed a reputation as a tough committee member on dissertation committees and as the guy that "once the door closed, was not afraid to ask the hard questions, with love and respect." Those early years in the department were a balance of fun and productivity. We worked hard and we played just as hard. The mantra was "We will take away all of your excuses for failure. We will give you what you need to succeed, but it will be up to you to justify our trust and investment in you."

I capitalized on the trust and support I felt from my colleagues when putting forth two new courses that would become staples of my teaching and research program. The first class I developed in 1995 was entitled, "Communicating with People with Physical Disabilities." Admittedly, the course was not my idea as I had always felt a bit apprehensive about teaching something like this thinking that such issues and concerns were too personal and that I could not talk about or conduct such research objectively. After one of our graduate students specifically requested the course from me in 1995, I thought I owed it to them and myself to at least try and began working on a pilot course focusing on communication issues and the physically disabled. You can see the development in its entirety in the published article in Appendix B, but, in general, this class ushered in a significant change in my teaching and research foci. I had been trained to be a Burkean rhetorical scholar and to teach and research such matters. Little did I know how significant that development would be for both me and our field. As you read the article at the end of this book, I hope you will be able to see the significance of that course.

I also wanted to take another stab at creating a class inspired by the one I had taught at IU Southbend focusing on aspects of Black America. After going through an intense curriculum development process, I settled on the course title "Black Communication Styles" and offered the first iteration of this class in 1996. The course was popular and over the next 15 years it would become a fixture in the department as a senior capstone synthesis experience. The course focused on the cultural and communication aspects relative to the Black style of communication, beginning with the African influences and ending with contemporary exigencies. The sample syllabus located in Appendix C of this text is a combination of this original class and the graduate class that would ultimately result from it. I dare say that both of these courses allowed me to teach and research in the areas that would ultimately become significant examples of my faculty profile. I am honored to have been one of the founding members of the National Communication Association Disability Issues Caucasus in 1998. I served as the second Chair and it was so profoundly rewarding to see issues of the differently abled highlighted at the national level in our discipline. It is fair to say that such issues received scant attention in our discipline in the 90's. It is also fair to say that without the encouragement of others to more fully explore these issues in my own work, I would not be the teacher or scholar that I am today.

You might not think that issues of race and ethnicity are particularly salient in the blind community and, of course, you would be wrong. Despite Ohio's negative reputation in the blind community, I continued my involvement and, in fact, increased it with the National Federation of the Blind (NFB) when I moved to Ohio. In 1994, I was chiefly responsible for the creation of a local chapter in Athens of which I am still a member. This was a particularly interesting time in the organization because discussions of race and ethnicity were quite prevalent. Likely a reflection of the larger societal trend towards identity politics some in the organization pushed for the formation of an interest group focused primarily on the unique experiences of Black members and other "underserved populations." The leaders of the organization vehemently fought this thrust and routinely reminded members that, for the most part, blindness was the primary issue with which the organization would concern itself with. There had also been significant racial and ethnic conflict in

Indiana, but I had conscientiously chosen to stay far away; however upon moving to Ohio, I learned about the time when there were two NFB chapters in the Cleveland area—one for Black members and one for white members. As a fairly new member and young professor, I thought it was important to chime in my two cents worth. Thus, after much discussion and some serious vetting, the article included in full below was published in the Braille Monitor in February 1994. It is an understatement to say that it received a great deal of attention, praise and disdain alike, but I believe it helped to focus the debate at a critical time in the organization and is demonstrative of my progress as a scholar in this area. Once again, I felt compelled to address the intersectionality of race, ethnicity and the differently abled, that had long been absent in my scholarly writing.

RACE AND REASON: A BLACK PERSPECTIVE ON A DARK ISSUE
By Dr. John W. Smith

From the Editor: Dr. John Smith is an Assistant Professor of Speech Communication at Ohio University. He is an active Federationist and a member of the board of directors of the NFB of Ohio. He has thought long and hard about the Federation and racial and ethnic relationships among Federationists. Here is what he has to say:

I often refer to myself as belonging to a double minority. I am a blind African American. This double minority status presents me with both obstacles and opportunities--fortunately, more opportunities than obstacles. Since joining the National Federation of the Blind, I have come to realize that many others share this distinction with me. It is from this perspective that I want to address the issue of race within the NFB.

First, let me explain why I am using the term African American. Of course, it is politically correct; but more important, some African Americans find the term "black" or "the blacks" offensive. However, African Americans active in the sixties insisted on being called "black" rather than "colored" or "Negro." Therefore, it seems okay to me to use the term. Some black Americans still prefer to have it that way. Throughout this article I will use the terms interchangeably. Strictly speaking, no one is really black or white. The correct terms of description are "caucasoid" or "negroid."

Racial differences have too often, and increasingly of late, preoccupied the communities in which we humans live. But we in the Federation must not allow the issue of race to fracture the unity and solidarity of our movement. We must address this issue openly and frankly and cut off its ugly head whenever and wherever we find it. Racial bigotry (regardless of which race practices it and regardless of whether the terminology used is nigger and honky, black and white, or African-American and Euro- American) is a poison that, left untreated, will corrupt the very essence of a person, group, organization, or movement. It will debilitate and destroy.

I want to dispel two myths about this issue as it relates to the Federation. Myth number one is that no racism exists in the NFB. I have heard well-meaning Federationists exclaim, "I have a hard time telling a person's race, especially those from the South." Can a blind person discriminate based on the sound of someone's voice? Yes, indeed. Sometimes we make bad choices based on erroneous information or at least incomplete information, e.g., someone sounds black or white or acts in accordance with the cultural stereotypes attributable to a given ethnic group. We as individuals choose (sometimes unintentionally or because we're not sure) to include or exclude this or that person from our circle of friends. I think this unintentional discrimination is easier to forgive than the intentional discrimination that occurs when we validate our information and knowingly choose to include or exclude on the basis of race, but it is still racism.

And if you think I am only talking about whites, you are wrong. Racism can be practiced by any group or individual. It comes from the caste of the mind, not the pigment of the skin. In some senses I believe that all of us to one degree or another are racists, because I define racism as the making of choices based on race. Such choices can be either positive or negative. They are positive when they are grounded in pride, mutual advancement, and the reinforcement of a sense of belonging and self-worth.

The problem occurs when we cease to concentrate on race- based pride, dwelling instead on our ignorance and bigotry concerning other people. I define bigotry as the belittling of another's race to enhance one's own race and culture. It's appropriate to have pride in one's own ethnic and cultural identity and achievements, but not at the expense of any other ethnic or cultural group.

If nothing else, our coming together as members of the National Federation of the Blind has demonstrated to all of us that we are simply people who cannot physically see. Despite what some have thought and written, we are first and foremost human beings with all of the shortcomings and inadequacies that plague mankind. Let us then agree as Federationists that, while it is possible for us to practice bigotry, we should make every effort not to do so.

The second myth is that everyone in the Federation is a bigot and that most of the organizational decisions made are racially motivated and designed to keep one group from succeeding in the movement. This classic song of victimology has become tiresome and evermore discordant in our society at large. I don't like to hear African American Federationists sing it, but sing it some of us do. In fact, some black Federationists are saying that we need a black caucus within the NFB. At the risk of being labeled an Uncle Tom, I want to go on record as strongly opposed to this idea. We have too many battles to wage as blind people to allow our energies and focus to be fractured. Besides, compared to the sighted, our numbers are few. Our common bond and burden are our blindness and society's misconceptions about it. The sighted see us as blind people first and then as black or white.

My fellow Federationists, we cannot afford to discriminate against each other. If (whether you are black or white) you are guilty of racial bigotry in your chapter or state affiliate, I urge you to rethink your behavior. Most social movements that have been destroyed have been torn apart from within. Rome was not built in a day, and it was not destroyed in a day either. Over the course of almost two centuries, its very foundations were pulverized and hammered to pieces by inner conflict and strife so that, when the barbarians came, there was little to overrun.

Our strength in the Federation is rooted in our unity of purpose and our capacity to bring undivided commitment and attention to issues affecting the blind. We have too much to fight for and against to allow ourselves to get bogged down in contentious matters that could divide us into warring factions. Those of you who are familiar with our history are aware of the civil war of the late 1950's. It was the greatest threat that our movement has ever faced, one that almost destroyed us. Let history not record that we had a second civil war, one based on racial conflict.

Those Federationists who claim to find racism in every corner of our movement should decide now whether or not to continue in it. Why should people who vehemently and unconstructively criticize the movement and its leaders remain in the organization? I suspect that down deep inside, even these few Federationists know in their hearts that in this movement we cannot be divided or separated into racial or ethnic units but are inextricably linked together by our blindness. They know that each victory and each defeat impacts the entire blind community, regardless of race, ethnicity, or cultural identity.

To all true Federationists I would say in the strongest possible terms: Never use racism as an excuse for lack of initiative or integrity. Among the attractions of this movement for me were the integrity of its leaders and the genuine commitment to working together of the rank-and-file members. It is this emphasis on honesty, openness, and unity that will continue to serve us well as we enter the twenty-first century. I challenge each one of us at every level of our movement to take a good, hard look at our attitudes about racism--not practicing it, not condoning it in others, and not using the claim of its existence in somebody else as an excuse for practicing it ourselves. Let us agree to continue to be united as one to ensure equality, security, and opportunity for all blind people. We can; we must; and I pray that we will.

I remember receiving a great deal of feedback about this publication and much of that feedback was colored by anger and frustration and, in other cases, by apprehension and exhilaration. Eventually, a committee was established to address issues of underserved populations in the organization with the emphatic directive that this could not just be used as a Black caucus or committee solely focused on racial issues.

Meanwhile, back in Athens, my first decade was preceding nicely due in large parts to the leadership of our school's director and other senior faculty.

In addition to the invitational culture of the school and the genuine enactment of inclusion and diversity, the director found ways to address my specific professional and faculty needs adroitly and effectively. It was also clear that the university was authentic in its desire to create an accessible environment and, even better for me, was willing to "put their money where their mouth was." Before I even arrived on campus, I received a letter basically telling me to list any equipment that I thought I would need to do my job and it would be purchased for me. It was there when I arrived alongside a promise to procure anything else I might need in the future. It was truly an amazing time for me as a differently abled faculty member in what I perceived as a special and unique school and university. One particular incident and experience best captures, for me, the effectiveness and genuine concern of our school director at that time. In 1995, I had been awarded one of the Outstanding New Teacher Awards by the Central State Speech Communication Association (CSSCA). It was a great honor and the meeting where I would receive my award was held in Indianapolis, Indiana. After discussions with my director about my travel plans, she confidently informed me that she herself would be my escort as she wouldn't miss it for the world. I knew these weren't just pleasantries or an offer originating from a sense of obligation, but were genuine expressions of her pride in my accomplishment. As we drove to Indianapolis on Interstate 70, we ran into a major thunderstorm and heavy rain that got so bad at one point my director confessed to me just how difficult it was for her to see. A silence fell over the car as we gritted through the storm for what felt like eternity. When the sunshine magically appeared again, my director said to me, "That was quite a storm, but I'm glad we were together and that we kept going." That statement epitomized our school culture and our director's commitment to excellence and inclusion.

I would go on to have several traveling experiences like these with our director and other colleagues. Fortunately I never felt like a burden or as someone who needed specific attention, but instead felt just like everyone else along for the ride – both literally and metaphorically. No matter how eventful the journey was, or in many cases became, I always felt at ease with my colleagues. I remember attending another CSSCA conference, this time in St. Louis, Missouri, accompanied by one of my colleagues who had agreed to travel to and from Athens with me. Our trek home started out simple enough with a short train ride to the St. Louis airport where we caught a direct flight back to Columbus. At that time, there was a bus service between Columbus and Athens which I frequented for obvious reasons and she preferred due to the high price of airport parking. Not but a few minutes into our ride back to Athens the bus broke down. It was a very warm day and it took almost two hours for us to finally get transportation back to Athens. But, again, we were together. We talked about school issues and got to know each other. I remember while sitting on that bus, waiting for our substitute, thinking to myself, "What a wonderful group of people that I have the privilege to work with and live with." I have made the trip from the Columbus airport to Athens more times than I can count, but to this day the most memorable trips remain this one and my very first because it was in these moments that I first considered leaving Southbend and later that I was reminded just how right that decision was.

Over the last twenty plus years, I have attended a lot of conferences and events with my colleagues, but few are as memorial as the one we attended in Las Vegas in 1995. Not long after registering for the conference I learned that a first-year faculty member in the department was also attending and thought this would be a great chance for us to get to know each other. One evening, we received a dinner invite by two of his colleagues and happily accepted. We erroneously thought that we would be taking taxis to the restaurant, but since the weather was so nice his colleagues suggested that we walk the 8 or 10 blocks to the restaurant. If you can picture these two tall men quickly moving down the street, closely followed and pursued by my colleague and I did I mention it was his first time walking with a blind person and this was neither the best terrain or experience for such an endeavor. The sidewalks were very narrow, littered with obstacles that seemed to just pop up out of nowhere (trees, bushes, poles, bicycles, etc.), and given that we were adjacent to the Vegas Strip, which extremely busy street traffic-wise. We were both a little nervous and, at once point, we both exclaimed, "Just how far is this place? And why are they walking so fast and so far ahead of us!" Needless to say, we finally caught up with them and had a great meal and fellowship together. We were more comfortable on the return trip and again I share this with you to demonstrate the kind of colleagues that comprised the special place where I worked and lived. To this day, we reminisce about that "long walk" and how much we learned about each other. In many ways, it was will always be a defining experience and aspect of our relationship.

I do want to be careful here, however, because there are no perfect people and no perfect faculty or departments. Two experiences occurred at faculty meetings that continued to remind me of my unique position and perspective in our school during those early years. At one particular faculty meeting, a dear colleague of mine (and they remain that way today), committed quite the blunder while discussing an upcoming job search. In reference to the position announcement itself, my colleague bluntly asked, "Why don't we go after somebody from a traditionally underrepresented group from the beginning and not just be content with add-ons?" I know the point they were making and I have no doubt that it was well-intentioned because in many ways this person was almost single-handedly responsible for attracting and maintaining many of the Black and international students in our program. Their reputation and commitment to real diversity was impeccable, but their use of the term "add-on" prompted someone to look at me and say, "Do you feel like an add-on?" As a blind person, I wish I could have seen the look on my friend's face when they recognized the implications of using that particular term in that particular context. I was stunned and a bit numb as we left the faculty meeting so I decided to send my colleagues an email letting them know that I did not feel like an "add-on" nor had I ever since joining them in 1993. My wonderful colleague sent a reply email that I wish I had saved to this day. More than just an apology, they spoke from a place of vulnerability and in-spired each of us to recommit ourselves to our school's culture and mission statement. I'm sure that neither of us have ever forgotten that experience and, in fact, several years later it was used in a positive way to make specific situa-tions even better. Equally salient in my memory is a faculty meeting when one of my colleagues decided to make a joke that clearly referred to the differently abled. The joke was not particularly funny and it was delivered so seamlessly that, at first, I did not grasp its potential damage and ignorance. But true to our culture, several of my other colleagues did. Here was yet another moment I wish I had my sight if only to see everyone's facial expressions. I found out later that several of my colleagues were so outraged that they went to this fac-ulty member and spoke up for me. To make a long story short, my colleague came to my office almost in tears to apologize to me directly and to clear the air in any way that was necessary. I appreciated and respected my colleague even more because I knew it was genuine and it has never happened again, at least not in my presence. What is my point here? Imagine these two scenarios without me in the room. You could argue that perhaps the two incidents would not have occurred, but I think they would have. As well-meaning as both of my colleagues were, my unique presence and position as a Black and blind colleague allowed for two significant, teachable moments that even faculty need sometimes. The lesson for me was equally powerful – if you surround yourself with the right people then they will fight your battles for you and not out of need but out of respect.

This might be a good time to talk about, specifically, how I do my job. I am frequently asked such questions and I think it is necessary to address some of them here. In terms of teaching, I hope that I have evolved in that I try to combine lecture with electronic demonstrations. One aspect of my teaching and imparting knowledge that I have found to be not just informative, but necessary, is to invite relevant contributors from relevant communities to address my classes. This has been particularly effective, I believe, and helpful in my differently abled course across the years (see Appendix B for the course documents). I firmly believe students learn best when they hear the narratives and experiences from people in the community or from those who have the specific differently abled ability that we are covering at the time. Technology has allowed me to utilize email submissions for assignments, but there are times when I give regular True/False, multiple choice-type quizzes and exams. When I do this, I invite proctors to come and keep an eye on the students, knowing human nature like we all do. Every professor in history has had their share of cheating or slacking, but I have never felt that I experienced any more or less of it because of my blindness. I will say that many of my students are tempted to spend far too much time on their cell phones and other gadgets, but I have learned over the years that this is not unique to my classes. I remember one incident in a public speaking class that occurred in about 1996 or so when I had put on a 15 or 20-minute video for the students to watch. At the time my office was located directly adjacent to the classroom. So after putting on the video, I went to my office to make a couple of pressing phone calls and make a few brief notes. I was only gone about ten minutes and I was literally right next door, but when I returned to the classroom only a handful of the twenty students remained. After the video, I told the three students to inform their friends that they hadn't gotten away with it and to expect an earful next class session. For a while I was furious that they had tried to take advantage of me and my blindness. When I arrived for the next class session, the first thing I noticed before even entering the room, was how quiet it was. I decided to milk it for all it was worth. So, I walked in and stood at the podium for a solid ten minutes before uttering a single word. The silence was deafening. As I hoped would happen, finally one of the students just had to explain herself. She said, "I didn't leave because you were blind. I left because the video was boring and I thought I knew the information already." Confession after confession followed thereafter and I seized the opportunity for another teachable moment. In my thirty years of teaching, this is the only incident like this that I can remember. But, I must tell you, I don't leave for long periods of time anymore because, as you know, "when the cat is away, the mice will play."

The obvious question is how does the publishing process work for me and the obvious answer is through a combination of hard work and libations to get the creative juices flowing. The more accurate answer involves the judicious help and support of people throughout my career – not unlike the scribes who were instrumental during my comprehensive exams. Each year since my arrival at Ohio University, I have been granted such an opportunity to hire someone, albeit I have to apply each year. With these capable undergraduates and my occasional hiring of graduate students and other assistants, I have managed to maintain a relatively consistent publishing record and line of research. In hindsight, I probably could have been much more productive if I had insisted on working with either a graduate student each year or a paraprofessional individual that was familiar with both the publishing process and academia in general. Be that as it may, I have utilized my administrative skills to maximize the contributions from my academic team over the years. My vita in Appendix A should give you a sense of both my productivity and contributions to our field to date. I intentionally chose not to bring any of my years of service from IU Southbend so that I could have more time to build up my publishing support team and get things in the pipeline. It was indeed a joy when I received my official letter informing me that I had been both tenured and promoted. I remember holding the letter in my hand after taking it out of my mailbox and literally zoning out for a few minutes in total excitement and exhilaration. Of course, I had not done it by myself, but together, we had accomplished our intended goal. By we, I mean my family, my support team, and my colleagues.

I recently had lunch with one of the more extraordinary undergraduate assistants from that first decade. Her name is Laura and I selected her when she was one of my first-year advisees. In her initial advising session with me in 1999, not only did she have a 4.0 GPA but there was something about her that indicated to me that she was wise beyond her years. Boy, was I right! She would go on to serve as the assistant that would work for me the longest and after taking a suggestion from me she would pursue her graduate degree in rehabilitation counseling. I eventually performed the wedding ceremony for her and her husband in 2005 and she remains an effective rehabilitation counselor to this day. We had so much fun reminiscing about those years, how our paths crossed, and where we both are today.

On a personal level, the 90's were a time of expansion for my family as well. When we moved to Ohio University in 1993, we were pregnant with our second child and this presented an enormous challenge in finding a doctor that would take on a new patient that would soon become two new patients. Once again, you can see God's hand at work. The husband of our director was an administrator for our medical school and he used his position and contacts to make it possible for us to get a doctor. Our second daughter, Joshelyn, was born in January 1994 and given the remarkable woman she has become today I am not surprised that her entry into the world was equally remarkable. Just five days before her arrival, Athens experienced its first huge blizzard of the season dumping 17 inches in one night and then followed by another 8 inches a few days later. The town and the university were closed for an entire week and the only approved travel was by the National Guard. Our doctor told us to inform them about my wife's condition and let them know that if the baby came early, they would have to come up the hill and get us. I remember trying to open my front door after the first deluge of snow and literally having to shovel a path from that front door down to my street. Fortunately for everyone involved, Joshelyn held off until the following week making it possible to get to and from the hospital without military escort although that would have admittedly made for quite the story. In 1995, my wife began a 13-month, intensive MBA program, complete with a 3 week trip out of the country. My children were only 5 and 1 but with the help of an excellent babysitter during the day, we managed to keep things together while my wife spent three weeks in Hungary. People have often asked and, unfortunately, assumed that blind people cannot be effective parents. Sadly, there have been times when peoples' blindness has been used as the sole basis for removing a child from their care. Yes, it was helpful that my wife was sighted, but I like to think that I made meaningful contributions to the raising and developing of our children, even as a blind father. One of the mantras that I promoted in our family was to ask my children, "How does Daddy see?" The right answer was, "With his hands and ears." Of course, that's not all I use, but I think it made the point with my girls. Still, there would be times that I would be out with my children and someone would exclaim, "What good children you are for taking care of your dad!" We would all chuckle and continue on our way.

The issue of race and my family in those early years would come up often likely as a result of being one of the few black families in a predominantly Caucasian town like Athens. I remember one of my daughters coming home literally in tears because she kept having that experience in some of her classes where everyone would look to and at her the instant issues of race were discussed. I remember telling her, "Get used to it, but you still don't have to like it nor play that game." My wife and I taught our children, both formally and by example, to see people as people first and not by their race or ethnicity.

Having said this, I often wonder if we should have exposed them to more culturally sensitive and educational opportunities. It was easy, I think, for them
to grow up in a generic and homogenized community like Athens and to
falsely assume that this was how the "real world" was. We had a few black
families that we fellowshipped with in those early years, but they eventually
moved away. I couldn't help but notice that when my children were around
our families in their predominantly Black, cultural context, they were not as
comfortable as they could or should have been.

All in all, however, the 90's were a wonderful time for me personally and
professionally. I established myself as a unique faculty member in this field of
Communication Studies and we established our family as a unique entity in
the community. We were active in church and I performed in a variety of clubs
and churches around town. That first decade laid the foundation for our time
in the 21st Century. I remember the Y2K hysteria. My wife and I decided, for
the one and only time, to attend a New Year's Eve party on December 31st,
1999. It was a party by one of my Black colleagues and it wasn't too far from
our house, just in case something did happen. Of course, all went well and our
kids and the babysitter survived each other nicely. As that first decade ended,
and as I sat in my office on September 11th, 2001, waiting to go and teach my
persuasion class, the world changed forever. As events unfolded, I told a student that was sitting in my office at the time, "The world and our lives will
never be the same after today." I had no idea how prophetic that statement
would be.

Chapter 4: After Tenure and Promotion—Embracing the 21st Century

I don't want to imply that changes and events in our school were comparable to what occurred on September 11th, 2001 in our country, but that year did usher in some significant occurrences in the School of Interpersonal Communication at Ohio University. For the first time ever, we decided to search for an administrator outside of our school and after a failed search in our first attempt, we were finally successful. The changes were immediate and significant. Eventually, our doctoral program would transition from a three year to a four-year program and we would also eliminate our one-year Master's program. In an attempt to more accurately reflect our new school culture and foci we also made the difficult decision to change our name from INCO to Communication Studies. Although these changes irrevocably altered our program, I'm sure that some would argue that, for the most part, these were positive changes for our school. In my opinion, they were ambivalent in some cases and less constructive in others. Was it purely coincidental that 2001/2002 seemed to usher in an era of less non-White graduate students in our graduate program? Was it similarly just a coincidence that, as we lost several non-

White members of our faculty we struggled to fill those positions with other traditionally underrepresented candidates? It struck me one day as I looked around during a faculty meeting and discovered that with the departure of my two Black colleagues, one due to retirement and one for a better opportunity, that I was the only one left. Our program was not an isolated incident as I became increasingly aware of more and more Black faculty leaving departments across campus. It was at this time when I began to feel isolated and felt the significant absence of peers who had cultivated a collegial community that I had become so accustomed to and, I dare say, depended on. After receiving tenure and promotion, I was approached by our interim director and asked to serve in one of the administrative roles in our program. This colleague had become our interim director after the sudden resignation of our long-time previous director. I remember that faculty meeting so vividly. It was fairly routine and innocuous until the end. With tears and disbelief, our director announced their resignation, left the room, and our then Dean of the College walked in to try to calm the waters. The unease and ambivalence was palpable and numbing. We had to make quick decisions, one of which resulted in the appointment of our colleague as interim director while we searched for a new director from outside of the school.

It is within this context that I assumed my administrative role as Associate Director of the Undergraduate Program. A full description of my responsibilities is available on my vita in Appendix A, but one of the overriding responsibilities for me in that position was to bring our enrollment of majors to a more manageable level. At that time we had close to 800 majors, but an optimal number for us was somewhere around 500. I was soon thrust into the position of the "bad guy" and had to quickly develop a level of comfortability with rejecting applications from students who did not meet our programmatic goals. I can still remember times when I would arrive at my office to find a group of rejected students outside my door, sometimes with their parents, seeking an opportunity to plead their case. I could only imagine what they thought, and probably said, when they found out that the "bad guy" was blind and Black. I vividly remember locking horns with several fathers of prospective students and having to stand my ground as to why I was rejecting their otherwise stellar child. Although this was a very stressful time for me as an administrator (my first such job after tenure and promotion), there was one incident that is indelible in my memory. One student seeking admittance into our program took the time to submit their application materials in both print and braille. It was an impressive application and, in some ways, I wish that I had saved it to this day. I remember meeting with them to inquire as to how they had been able to get the materials in this format and what motivated them to take such extraordinary measures. I was taken aback with the simplicity of their answer as they spoke of the importance of always knowing your audience and adjusting your message accordingly. Needless to say, although the slots were few and very difficult to get, this student was enthusiastically admitted. I enjoyed working in this capacity for our interim director and he never pressured me to reconsider any of my decisions. When times got really difficult, both with students and parents, he stood by me throughout the entire process.

While the Black community was disintegrating at the University in terms of both numbers and efficacy, the differently-abled community was maturing and becoming more viable. It would be generous to say that efforts to address and support the differently abled population were quite anemic when I first arrived at Ohio University in 1993. By late 2002, we had made significant and positive gains in this area. We now had a full-time person responsible for these issues and, in fact, my wife had been one of the finalists for that job. We also formed a diverse university-wide committee comprised of relevant representatives from the university community to address issues facing the differently abled population across campus. I began to see substantial changes and was often granted significant input in terms of addressing physical, curricular, and programmatic issues relevant to the differently abled community on our campus. We recruited and welcomed more differently abled students and seemed genuinely committed to providing support for them in all aspects of their experience at Ohio University. The difference was particularly striking for people who'd been on campus throughout this transition period. One particular student who completed their undergraduate in the late 1990's and later returned to work on their Ph.D. in cultural studies, noted that the improvement in services was a motivating factor in their choice to return to OU. Over time our relationship flourished and stands as a symbol of the university's commitment to disability issues. We served on search committees together and frequently collaborated to make Ohio University a more accessible place for differently abled persons. Years later when serving as the chair of a committee charged with finding a new administrator for our disability services office, they would be one of the finalists. As I interviewed them for the position I caught myself beaming with pride at both the talent of my colleague and the emergence of the campus services I helped build.

It was wonderful to be able to share relevant topics and conversations with someone who had an obvious disability like myself. Even though I was a faculty member and this individual was a graduate student in our cultural studies program, we bonded over this unique context. We also bonded over a series of interesting incidents shared during our time at Ohio University. One night after leaving one of the local bars, we stood outside waiting for our ride when a young woman approached us. As I remember it, it was the Thursday before one of our infamous Halloween weekends in Athens and the sidewalks were filled with students and visitors eager to get the weekend started early. The conversation started off relatively benign as she asked us some fairly broad and routine questions, like our names, what we were doing out, and what we did on campus. The conversation took a turn when the young woman inquired as to whether or not I was "really blind." After assuring her that I was, she grew quite belligerent and loud and implied that I should stop pretending to be blind. Undeterred by the repeated assurances offered by my friend and I, she got right in my face and used several expletives to convey to me how much of a liar I was. Though we maintained our tough exteriors, it definitely got scary at some points as she continually raised her voice and vehemently implored me to stop joking. After repeated attempts to convince her that I was indeed legitimately a blind man, she just said, "I don't believe you," turned, and ran away. To this day, my friend and I routinely revisit that night and share our experience with others. One other aspect of our relationship often came up as well. It was the dilemma about could a temporarily able-bodied individual really ever comprehend what it was like to be an obvious member of the differently abled community? This debate still rages as others attempt to research and write in this area. My colleague and I firmly believe that there are experiences and contexts that temporarily able-bodied individuals (TABS) would never be able fully understand or appreciate as an outside team member. As you might expect, some people are quite offended by this assertion and others accept it and understand it. I felt compelled to participate on a conference panel addressing this topic, fully understanding that there will probably never be a right answer that fully addresses this dilemma. I believe that the text of this short paper gives you some idea of this issue faced by me and others, both on and off campus:

(Dis)ability Membership

Code switching as defined by Martin and Nakayama (2013) is a technical term in communication that refers to the phenomenon of changing language, dialects, or even accents. One reason they argue that groups engage in code switching is to "avoid accommodating others" (p. 257). I would like to discuss how persons with disabilities (the "in" group) and especially those with more obvious physical disabilities (i.e. blind and visual impairment, deaf and hard of hearing, and mobility impairments) utilize this phenomenon to separate and accentuate their uniqueness from the able bodied community and those with less obvious disabilities. How is this "in" group communication enacted to ensure credible membership in this exclusive community, and what are the implications of this enactment for successful and effective dialogue between communities? I further contend that there is a non-verbal aspect to this phenomenon as well and that particular communication contexts encourage the enactment of code switching.

"The Club" and the Problem

"In her work on code switching, communication scholar Karla Scott (2000) discusses how the use of different ways of communicating creates different cultural contexts and different relationships between the conversants. Based on a series of interviews with black women, she notes "the women's shared recognition that in markedly different cultural worlds their language use is connected to identity" (Martin & Nakayama, 2013)

This focus of Dr. Scott is the more common way that code switching is generally discussed and experienced i.e. racial and ethnic issues often focusing on the black community. My contention in this brief discussion is that it occurs in a variety of cultural settings and especially the community of those with disabilities. My experience has been that it functions more as an exclusionary tactic as opposed to an accommodating goal of conversance.

So what is "the club"? It is comprised of those of us who are in what I call the "big three" as stated earlier blindness and obvious visual impairment, deafness and obvious hard of hearing, and mobility impairment and obvious developmental disabilities. I emphasize obvious because the inability to hide the disability is a key ingredient in both the status and contextual acceptance in this special "club/in group". It is a unique culture with specific guidelines for membership e.g. are you disabled enough to really claim membership and what are the implications of these often unspoken requirements?

Allow me a brief personal story. While at a conference some years ago my friend and I returned to our hotel room and on our way encountered a mutual acquaintance. As we begin to talk it became clear that our acquaintance had a great deal of sight and it was also clear to me that my friend either had forgotten this or never knew it. He immediately lapsed into group code speak with comments like "you really have to be blind to understand" and "it's a visual thing, you know" and "isn't braille great?" After our mutual acquaintance had left, he shared with me how he could not believe that she had so much sight and how it was probably very difficult for her to really understand our world. I strongly disagreed with him and told him so but I chose not to pursue the conversation any further at that point.

This example is one of several that I have experienced in a variety of contexts and it highlights the problem of this "in group" communication that often occurs as a way of excluding others. Unfortunately, it is often intentional and quite rude but I understand why it happens. Many of us with disabilities have used it to try to maintain a safe space away from pity and paternalism and well-meaning people and as a way of bonding and sharing unique experiences. But the problem goes deeper because it often makes the "outsider" feel quite defensive and excluded and in many ways it demonstrates the very same thing that those of us in the community fight against i.e. feeling shut out, having others try to speak for us and often being felt like people would rather communicate with the disability instead of the person with the disability. Finally, the problem is also not just limited to communication between people with disabilities and TABS (temporarily abled bodied) but it also rears its ugly head when there is a diverse meeting of even members of the "big three" and one of those groups dominate the context both in terms of numbers and or philosophy. Simply put, I have observed tension and contention when people from the deaf community dominate a particular environment or people from the mobility impaired community dominate it. In short, everyone believes that their part of "the club" and more importantly, their communication issues relative to their population, should dominate particular contexts.

Some Possible Solutions

In his article "Pushing Forward: Disability, Basketball, and Me" the author Ronald Berger comes face to face with the "insider/outsider" dilemma as a result of raising his daughter that has cerebral palsy:

Having moved many years ago from Los Angeles to the Midwest, a land of few Jews, I have grown accustomed to living as an "outsider," an ideal place for a sociologist who observes. I was not quite prepared, however, to be treated as an outsider by other people with disabilities. I do not know why I was so naïve. When I first began reading the disability studies literature, dominated these days by writers who have disabilities, I was confronted with the question, "What are you doing here?" (Branfield, 1998, 1999). It was as if I was being told: You who are able bodied, who are not disabled, need not apply. This is our terrain. Please leave us alone. We do not need or want your help. Research by the nondisabled is exploitative—"nothing about us without us" (Charlton, 1998). (Berger, 2004).

Unfortunately, this is not a unique occurrence for people like Berger and I will not spend the time here to go into all the details of the article but suffice it to say that it has become a bigger challenge for a number of reasons in recent years. There is now more attention on people with disabilities and much of that is positive but it also brings the necessity to include the diverse worlds of people with disabilities i.e. it is not a simple cut and dry existence like some books or films would like to have us believe. As I stated earlier, I hope that you will get the article for yourself but I thought it was instructive to include here some of the solutions proposed by Berger:

I was quite frankly angered that my motivation was being questioned. I felt on the defensive and quickly sought to legitimate my presence. I told them about Sarah—she is the reason I am here. Do you not think it is important to understand why some people with disabilities are managing to do well? Do you not want people with disabilities to do well? Of course they did, and with this my presence was accepted. We began to reach a meeting of the minds, a rapprochement, a feeling of camaraderie that we were all in it together. A little personal disclosure goes a long way.

As I read further in the disability studies literature, I was pleased to come across welcoming voices (Darling, 2000; Duckett, 1998). To turn away the nondisabled, some said, is to reproduce the same patterns of exclusion those who are disabled have been fighting against. In an article on disabled people's opinions about disability research, I learned that some did not want to leave the field in the hands of a small cadre of academics with disabilities who may have a professional agenda of their own that does not represent the interests of the diverse constituency of the disabled (Kitchen, 2000). This field of inquiry should be open to all. They ask only that researchers approach the topic from a "disabled-friendly" point of view—that they are able to empathize with people with disabilities (verstehen), not misrepresent the experiences of the disabled, and use their research to advance the principle of equality for the disabled (Kitchen, 2000, p. 36; also see Darling, 2000). (Berger, 2004).

In my mind, this really sums up the issues but I want to conclude with two final observations and potential solutions. First, to those who may feel excluded at times- try not to get too defensive and try to understand the "insider/outsider" dilemma and double consciousness that is often experienced by those in traditionally underrepresented and marginalized groups. Often, the exclusionary tactic is not intentional or personal and in fact it is necessary; albeit I will admit rude and fraught with risks. As a TAB or non-member of the dominating group in a particular context, a simple stepping back and objective inquiry might be helpful at times.

Second, however, those of us with disabilities have to be aware of our accountability in aspects of these communication exchanges as well. This was brought home to me in a very arresting way at the end of a class presentation that I did for a colleague at my university. After spending about 45 minutes talking about what "outsiders" should do to make communication between those of us with disabilities and those of us without more effective, a female in the back of the room with a clear international accent said "you've spent all this time telling us what we should do but what is your role and accountability in these situations?" I must tell you I was caught off guard by the excellent comment and question and it has caused me since to be mindful of the transactional nature of communication. It is a give and take and therefore those of us as members of the "big three" need to do all in our power to lessen the tension and not to do things to throw additional road blocks in the paths of those that could be potential allies. Additionally, as I did with my friend, we have a responsibility not to let other members in our group enact ineffective and destructive code switching tactics. I firmly believe that more significant research and conversation in this area is necessary.

Eventually, I would serve on the dissertation committee of my graduate student colleague and perform the wedding ceremony to his lovely bride on the steps of our campus chapel. It was so rewarding to see my colleague finally obtain employment and validation for all of his hard work and extensive intellectual development and capabilities. It is an understatement to say that I miss his presence around here, to this day, and I look forward to future conversations and collaborative efforts with him. Before I leave this area, I think it is important for me to document another experience that occurred in one of my classes. I had a blind student in my disability class and one of the assignments required a scholarly paper, complete with appropriate citations and documentation. After dragging their feet for some time concerning this assignment, the student told me that, because of their blindness, they would probably not be able to complete the assignment. I was incredulous, especially since I was blind myself, and knew that the assignment could be easily completed. I brought the student to my office and we had one of those "Come to Jesus" conferences. I could not believe that this student would try to pull this with me. I informed them, in no uncertain terms, that failure to complete this assignment would be detrimental to their overall success in this course. As the student left my office, I thought to myself, "How many times have they tried this with other faculty? And how many times have they been successful in promoting this as a legitimate excuse?" I have no doubt that they had tried it before and probably had been quite successful. It is my hope that in this case my blindness positively influenced and helped to contribute to the future success of this student. Talk about knowing your audience! Needless to say, they wrote and submitted an excellent research paper.

I increased my exposure to and involvement with the broader differently abled community in Ohio by submitting an application to be considered as a member of what was then called the State Consumer Advisory Council (CAC) of the Ohio Rehabilitation Services Commission (RSC) from 1994-2000. My involvement on this council lead to a natural commitment to serve on the Ohio Governor's Council on People with Disabilities. It was an honor to be appointed by Governor Taft for a three-year term on this council from 1998-2001. These two service opportunities helped me keep issues relative to the blind and visually impaired in the minds and on the agenda of Ohio's differently abled community writ large. This was important to me because I have always felt that issues of the blind and visually impaired can easily be lost in broader differently abled discussions and conversations. Even at Ohio University, it was frustrating to have conversations about accessibility often limited to mobility impaired contexts, i.e. ramps, curb cuts, and difficult terrain. Admittedly, these are very important issues and clearly worthy of attention, but I wanted to make sure that issues of the blind and visually impaired received equal attention by my presence at the table and in the room.

As you might expect, I increased my involvement with the NFB of Ohio and I was so honored to receive the National Blind Educator of the Year Award in 2004. Eventually, I would be elected as President of the NFB of Ohio in 2008. My first column for our affiliate newsletter sought to clarify both who I was and what I felt I could contribute to the organization at the time of my election.

From the President's Desk
by J. Webster Smith

Transitions are rarely easy, but they can be very exciting. In fact, I recently read something that said roughly, every exit is an entrance for new opportunities and adventures. I was so touched by this statement that I have put it on my cell phone message.

I sat with some ambivalence as Barbara Pierce delivered her valedictory address at the end of our convention on Sunday, November 2, 2008. Thankfully, Barbara will be with us both physically and in spirit for years to come, but her exit from the presidency does usher in a new era of leadership. Like many of you I have observed her leadership and marveled at her ability to perform the duties of this office, often apparently effortlessly. We have been blessed to have her guidance and love for twenty-four years, so I know that some of you who are reading this are experiencing ambivalence as well. First, I know you join me in thanking Barbara for her years of service to this organization and for her attention to detail in performing the duties of this office. More important, however, let's thank her for doing it with graciousness and love and genuine concern for our Ohio Federation family.

I have big shoes to fill, but I hope that I do not sound conceited when I say I believe I am ready for the task. Whenever I have needed the right people in my life and whenever I have been prepared for the right assignment, God has made it possible. I'm sure some of you are wondering who I am and, more important, what I bring to the table at this critical time in our movement.

Who Am I?

I am a father and a family person, and I love my wife and two daughters with all my heart. I've been married since 1986, and because of my wife Regina I am who I am today. She keeps the home fires burning, provides stability, and allows me to travel and do what I feel I've been called to do. She has always been a quiet, reserved individual who detests the limelight, but I think the statement "still waters run deep" best characterizes her personality and her perspective on life. Through the years you've read much about my daughters Ebony and Joshelyn. Ebony is in her first year at Ohio University, majoring in interior design, and Joshelyn is in her first year of high school, majoring in anything she can get into. These women are the joy of my life and the center of my world.

I am a fighter and a futurist. I was a wrestler in high school, and I had a reputation for being tenacious and one who fought till the bitter end. I will bring that same tenacity to the office of president. I will fight for what is right for blind Ohioans, and I will fight for those who either have lost their fight or don't feel empowered to fight. I don't intentionally go looking for fights, but I am a futurist in that I like to see the big picture and I like to move the ball down the field. I love to play chess and checkers, and as you know, to be successful at those games, one must anticipate as many future moves as possible for both oneself and one's opponent. My futuristic tendency allows me to be far-sighted, trying to be proactive rather than reactive.

Finally, I am a performer, a professor, and a partner. By performer I mean a musician, public speaker, and preacher. I've been a professor at the university level since 1983 and since 1993 at Ohio University, where I teach in the School of Communication Studies. By partner I mean I'm a team player, and I have no interest in being a lone ranger leader or dictator.

What Do I Bring to the Table?

I bring continuity and commitment. I want to continue the consistency that our movement in Ohio has enjoyed through the years. As first vice president since 1994, I have been a part of that consistency, and I want it to continue. I want to ensure that the NFB of Ohio is a place of stability and strength and that our positions are communicated effectively and persuasively. I want to continue our presence and prowess in the disability community in general and the blindness community in particular. We have established a reputation for integrity and credibility and the ability to get things done thanks to Barbara Pierce and Eric Duffy, and I want to keep that going.

I am committed to our philosophy and principles. We are changing what it means to be blind every chance we get, and I'm committed to the idea that blind people can do anything they want to do with proper training and opportunities. I've been a Federationist since 1990, and I've never been more committed than I am today. I attended my first national convention in Charlotte, North Carolina. in 1992, and I made up my mind then that I would give my life to this movement, so I am here for the duration, and I'm committed to our programs and our policies. My leadership style may be different from Barbara's, but my commitment to all that is the NFB of Ohio will be the same.

I bring education and enthusiasm. By education I mean both formal and informal. I don't want to be snobbish here, but I think that I have been able to use my years of formal education effectively in the real world. My formal education has taught me to be a facilitator and a problem solver. I think these skills will come in handy in this new job. I am enthusiastic about the capacity of blind people to do anything in life they want to do. I've traveled a great deal, and I've met a lot of people. In short, I have had and continue to have an exciting life that I think allows me to convince other blind people that they can have the same kind of experience. Research demonstrates that communicating enthusiastically and energetically can be contagious. Because I believe in this movement and the limitless capacity of blind Ohioans, I won't have any problem communicating all things NFB-O enthusiastically and energetically. Of course I will want to make sure that this excitement and enthusiasm are balanced by substance and purpose.

I bring organizational skills and an opportunity-friendly leadership style. I value organization and efficiency, and I take great pride in putting it all together. I also enjoy creativity and innovativeness. It's often difficult to keep the interest of this new generation, but I think that, as a movement and organization, we must try. My predecessor has made this job easier for me because of her meticulous attention to detail and superb organizational skills. I want to build on those and add my own creativity. I am one who likes to delegate tasks, and you might say that I enjoy discipling others. Discipleship requires time and commitment and a willingness to step in and not just pull people along but walk with them every step of the way. I want to give our members opportunities to work in our movement, but I want to make it clear that I will expect them to seize those opportunities and be positive contributors to our purpose and mission. For example, I want committees that get things done, and I want an infusion of new blood and faces.

That's who I am and what I believe I bring to this office. I am not perfect, and I will depend on the efforts of my board of directors and other leaders in this organization to ensure our success as a family. This is a we operation, and we need as many committed individuals as possible to help make our collective strength that much more evident. For the next two years I will try to be the best CEO I can be. I will try to guide with love and affection and genuine concern for all of you. I pledge to be the best president I can be. I pledge to continue our success, to be committed to our philosophy and programs, to educate others about who we are and what we want, and to provide opportunities for leadership and input that will be in the best interests of the NFB of Ohio. Together we can make it work, and I might add, work very well.

I was honored to serve two terms as president of this wonderful organization and it allowed me to make a difference in the lives of many blind and visually impaired Ohioans. In 2009, our National Convention was held in Detroit, Michigan and we ended up fourth in the nation in terms of our attendance, which was a great accomplishment for our affiliate and my administration. One highlight of that effort was that we were able to charter a bus that traveled from Cincinnati, making stops in Dayton and Toledo, on our way to the Detroit convention. I had a fundraising concert in Athens and, because of that effort, we raised enough money to make that bus trip free to all of the members that rode on it. We ended up registering 130+ Ohioans for that convention and, I dare say, it put a big smile on my face. It was a lot of work, but it was so gratifying. It was a balancing act to effectively perform my duties as affiliate president and to maintain my effectiveness as a university professor. Throw in my role as a father and husband and it is fair to say that 2008-2012 was a very busy time for me. The following article from the university paper, The Athens Post, best captures this event and time period in my life.

Blind professor holds concert to benefit national conference
By Jessie Cadle

In the blind community, there is a 70 percent unemployment rate. Dr. J. Webster Smith, an associate professor of communications who has been blind since birth, considers himself blessed to be employed and has devoted his life to giving back to others.

"I'm committed to helping people help themselves," said Smith, who is president of the National Federation of the Blind of Ohio. "I want to inspire (others) to do good and be better. I think I was put here to do that."

Smith, along with the help of local musicians Donny Boggs, Wayward Ridge Band and Double Shot, will present the Third Annual Sunday with Dr. FeelGood and Friends May 22 at the Athens Community Center.

The event is a benefit concert for the NFB of Ohio. Earnings from Dr. FeelGood and Friends will help finance trips to this year's NFB conference in Orlando, Fla.

"When I attended my first national conference in 1992, it was eye opening, no pun intended. When you are not around blind people, you forget there are all varieties of people who just happen to be blind," Smith said. "For me, joining the organization felt like coming home."

In past years the federation sponsored trips to the national conference for some of its members. However, the amount NFB of Ohio receives each year plummeted from about $500,000 to $30,000 when one corporate sponsor slashed funding in the summer of 2009.

Without financial assistance, many who are living on small salaries would not have the opportunity, Smith said.

The event idea stemmed from Smith's side career as Dr. FeelGood. He has produced three gospel CDs and is in the process of completing another album. Smith is also a preacher.

"All of them are about communicating," he said. "After you come to performances or speeches, if you can leave there feeling better about yourself ... man, I've done my job."

Smith utilizes all avenues to spread his message of being positive, maximizing potential and working to help others.

Smith's general purpose biography says, "he firmly believes that our differences can be our strengths and that many people live more for affirmation than bread and that we are each responsible to all for all."

Smith's message affects his students. He teaches classes ranging from Communications 110 to Black Communication Styles to a class he created himself, Communications with People with Physical Disabilities.

He has also written two books for his classes and is working on a third — an autobiography.

"When I think of Dr. Smith, I think that my family knows who he is," said Ashley Laber, a senior studying organizational communication, who has had three classes with him. "He is just one of those professors that I talk about."

Many of Smith's students have immense respect for him, but his laid-back and trusting teaching style, laced with practical advice based off of his life experiences, sets him apart, she said.

"Maximize every opportunity in the most positive way you can, and then do all you can to help others maximize their opportunities, too," Smith said. "If you can do that — wow, what a combination."

The 21st Century ushered in an era of technological advancement that was extraordinary to say the least. From talking computers to amazing phones, these technologies made my life and the lives of the differently abled even more manageable and opened doors long closed to us. The software for my computer allowed me to be on equal footing with my colleagues and, along with my braille ability, ensured my effectiveness as a professor at the undergraduate and graduate levels. I remember telling someone shortly after the release of the iPhone that I would probably never have a real use for it. Boy, am I happily mistaken. There are now apps that allow a blind and visually impaired person to know when the lights are on or off, identify the different denominations of dollar bills, identify specific colors of clothing, and even locate buildings and businesses with the swipe of a finger. Add to this the ability and capacity to read documents (even handwritten ones) is truly amazing. The capacity of the iPhone in the classroom was equally powerful. From the development and presentation of PowerPoints to the ability to surf the internet immediately and on the spot, the iPhone and other technologies like this have not only equaled the playing field, but allowed the blind and visually impaired professor to effectively address the technological needs of present day students. I will admit that I am probably not as technologically competent as some of my other blind and visually impaired brothers and sisters, but the technology has helped me to foster a classroom learning environment that I hope is comparable to those experienced by my students in other educational contexts. When they placed that initial computer on my desk at IUSB in 1992, little did I know how impactful such technologies would become in my life and in our world in the 21st Century.

Technological developments such as the iPhone also made my daily tasks far more manageable. Now when handouts are presented in faculty meetings and other public forums, I can quickly read the information and digest it just as my colleagues do and with the same speed and immediacy. Even though I have the capacity in my office to read and print materials in either braille or regular typeface, these technologies have given me a level of immediacy I had not experienced before. I must hasten to add, though, that while these technologies are extraordinary, and, I must admit, I still don't know how they truly work sometimes, it is not just the technologies that have made me more independent, but my attitude and training and experiences as a blind person in general, and a blind professor specifically. Years ago I spent hours in my classroom before the start of the semester to get a sense of the space, but now I have an app on my phone that allows me to instantaneously survey the space and give me meticulous details about the classroom and those in it.

One of the main reasons I came to Ohio University was to teach and advise graduate students. In recent years, I have done more graduate teaching and I guess it's safe to say now I am a senior faculty member. I do find it interesting and necessary to have an extended conversation with my graduate students, usually in the first week of the class focusing on what their experience will be like with a blind faculty member. There are different dynamics and, admittedly, it can take some adjusting to at times. I'm sure that some graduate students who rely on nonverbal feedback find it more difficult to adjust; I'm sure that hand raising and head nodding occur out of sheer habit and repetition; and I'm also sure that they leave my classroom with a different experience and one that has better prepared them to work with differently abled persons in the future. Although I enjoy teaching undergraduate students, I truly relish the opportunity to work with graduate students. I typically try to give graduate students more email assignments and interaction, which allows me the most immediate opportunity for feedback and input. I try to only have the most competent undergraduate students serve as scribes and readers for those graduate papers. I continue my frequent involvement and invitations to additional voices and presentations, even in those graduate classes, to balance the lack of nonverbal expectations and to promote diverse voices, perspectives, pedagogies.

In addition to teaching graduate students, I have found the relationship of the advisor and advisee to be particularly gratifying and rewarding over the past 15 or 20 years. I have had the pleasure of codirecting two dissertations and directing three to successful completion. Ironically, (or maybe not so much) my first graduate advisee in the late 90's was a Black male and it was so rewarding to see him not only successfully defend his dissertation but to hear the joy in his voice when he picked me up from the airport one day and exclaimed, "I am going to take that job!" Again, not to be stereotypical, but we literally wrote that dissertation week by week, meeting and eating that great Athens fried chicken that I alluded to earlier. My most recent advisee, was a Black male who, in no uncertain terms told me and our graduate director that the only reason he was coming to our program was to work with me. He wanted to work with another Black male and, sadly, there are so few of us in the field of Communication Studies. His arrival and four year stay with us was both comforting and disruptive at times. During his first year, a particularly controversial and poisonous rhetorical exchange occurred between him and another one of our graduate students outside of class. I am grateful that I have had very few of these kinds of racially tinged issues and developments during my time here, but this one was particularly disappointing and disruptive. It highlighted the issue of race or the lack thereof in our school and at the university in general. It is safe to say that my advisee was not just "pro-Black," but it seemed to me, at times, that "Black" and "White" colored many of our conversations and observations. It is safe to say that those conversations kept the issue fresh in my mind even perhaps when I didn't want it to be. However, what a joy it was to walk across that stage with my advisee and hood him after the successful completion of his degree. Even though the number of Black faculty at OHIO were shrinking, the university made a major step when it hired it's first Black President in 2004. I can still remember a meeting during the first year of his presidency that seemed more like a Black community rally than a formal meeting with a university president. The energy and positive view of the future was palpable in that room. Many thought that his hiring would refocus issues of diversity and race and ethnicity on campus and to some degree I think it did. But, to the President's credit, he seemed to be always conscientious of being the President of the entire university and not just one segment of it. As you might expect, however, this approach was disappointing to some and reassuring to others.

In 2012, I got the chance to offer my Black rhetoric course, which I had been trying to offer for several years at the graduate level but could never generate enough interest. Not only did the class make, but it was a rousing success. I am including the entire syllabus in Appendix C, and I am pleased to say that it will be updated, as I will get to offer the class again in 2019. Here is the relevant class overview and objectives, though, as a teaser:

I have wanted to teach this course at the graduate level since my arrival at Ohio University in 1993. I tried to offer it twice before, but unfortunately, the class failed to garner the necessary interest and thus, it is an understatement to say that I am very excited to be able to offer it this semester. For a number of years, I taught a version of this class at the undergraduate level and I entitled it Black Styles of Communication. That course focused on significant Black orators and their roles in the historical and cultural development in our society. Additionally, we examined the role of the Black church, the influence of slavery, the impact of sports and entertainment and hip-hop culture within that same context. The class was then known as a Tier III class which was designed to be a synthesized capstone class for graduating seniors. I enjoyed teaching that class, but I always wanted to offer much of its content as well as additional material at the graduate level.

Our focus for this course will be more theoretical in nature and more topical versus chronological. To this end, our main objectives include 1) Examining relevant literature and research that has contributed to and continues to inform our understanding of the rhetorical, methodological, and pedagogical exigencies involved in the study of Black Rhetoric. Please note that I am purposefully using the term Black for a number of reasons and I am in strong agreement with Cummings and Daniel who "recognize that 'African American' is the preferred term to 'black'; however, to use the latter term is to deny other people of African descent their role in this communication phenomena. Therefore, both terms will be used." 2) To examine those principles, nuances, and historical/cultural developments that have helped to create and maintain the "Black style of communication", 3) To expand our knowledge of and appreciation for this unique area of research and to perhaps make future recommendations for study in this area.

I view these graduate seminars as works in progress. Therefore, we will add appropriate reading materials as warranted, and utilize appropriate input when necessary (e.g. guest lecturers, field trips, and electronic presentations).

I have found that discussions of race and ethnicity and other relevant and often controversial topics proved to be more effective at the graduate level. I can understand that these are not easy topics to discuss and they have always been difficult for my undergraduate students, but my graduate classes have yielded some very rich conversations in these areas. In either case, I try to make the environment inviting for all. There were some heated discussions in that 2012 class that spilled over into our post-class environment at a local watering hole. To say that the class was diverse is an understatement. If memory serves me correctly, the 13 students consisted of three Black American females and one Jamaican female. There were also two African males and one Black American male. The other six students were all Caucasian – half male and half female. I dare say that there were times when I could literally feel the apprehension and hesitancy of my Caucasian students, especially as the volume of conversations rose and the language became indeed quite colorful. I would be remiss if I did not acknowledge the physical and emotional toll these classes can have on you, no matter how intellectually exhilarating they may be. You may be able to tell by the topics outlined in the sample syllabus how some of those conversations both developed and expanded at times.

One memorable topic and class session erupted as a result of a discussion of an article that focused on "the Angry Black Woman." As the class conversation heated up, it soon became very personal between a Black male and a Black female. This personal dialogue continued after the class and, at some point, a yelling match ensued and left the majority of the class in ambivalence at best and distraught at worst. The argument ultimately spilled out into the street and I really thought that these two would have to be physically separated. I had the utmost respect for both of them and so trying to be a referee was physically and emotionally draining. I am not sure to this day that they ever resolved their personal conflict and, yes, this an extreme example from that class, but there were other incidents like this (albeit not as volatile) that would occur from time to time.

Before I leave this area, though, I must tell you of a particular tactic that I used for some of my Black Styles of Communication class at the undergraduate level. In those early years of that class, I would intentionally alter my appearance and vocal delivery in the first week of the class to send a particular message or perception to my students. Sometimes I would dress in African garb and speak with a clearly African accent. Sometimes I would dress in Jamaican garb and accompany it with the appropriate vocalics. There was even one time when I put on a cowboy hat and as much Southern garb as possible and equipped myself with a very heavy Southern dialect. This was intentional for the first week and then, in the second week, I would come to class "just as myself" to see the reactions of my students. It seemed to work every time. They really bought my altered persona in that first week and it lead to perceptions about me as a person and, I dare say, a potential instructor. As you might expect, it became more difficult to continue this as students spread the word and the class gained in popularity, but I had so much fun doing it for about three or four years.

In addition to graduate teaching and advising, I've enjoyed the role of committee member and competent senior faculty member at all levels of our school. For the most part, my blindness has never, to my knowledge, kept me from being considered for leadership positions in the school or in our college. There was one incident, though, that I shall never forget and would like to document here for obvious reasons, I hope. As I discussed earlier, I have been blessed to have undergraduate assistants working for me each year and some of them served for me in two- or three-year increments. One of the things that I stressed with them is the issue of confidentiality – making it clear that what is said or read in this office, stays in this office. Students are required to sign a legal document pledging their confidentiality and to ease this burden on them I have always tried not to expose them to really sensitive and confidential materials. One of our practices is to circulate promotion and tenure letters and evaluations among the faculty, seeking input and feedback on relevant cases. To this day, I don't know how the rumor started, but someone implied that some of the sensitive material might have gotten out and as a result of my reader/assistant. I knew without a doubt that this was not the case and I thought it necessary to respond firmly to such an accusation. I believe I made the right decision as this kind of matter has never surfaced again. As I look back on that incident, I think it was a wise decision to reassure my colleagues that just because I did things differently, doesn't mean I didn't take issues of confidentiality very seriously. How about the 21st century! Now, because of my new phone app, I could read those letters without any assistance. However, this was the first time my blindness had the potential to be a major issue of concern, and not necessarily in a positive way.

Back on the home front, it has been a joy to see my daughters matriculate through Ohio University and obtain their undergraduate degrees. I think, for the most part, they have navigated the isolating world of Athens and found ways to validate their racial and cultural heritage. I would not dare to speak for them and, as I said earlier, I do wish in hindsight that we had intentionally exposed them to more salient racial and cultural experiences. They are now balanced and mature young women complete with their own unique personalities, life goals, and objectives. I am pleased that we fostered an environment that allowed them to make their own choices and to develop their own worldviews. Admittedly, some of their views are diametrically opposed to mine, but I'm okay with that. My wife, Regina, after receiving her MBA from the College of Business at Ohio University, continues to work as a Chief Financial Officer (CFO) of an agency here in Athens. We did have some family experiences with two or three other Black families in the late 1990's and early 2000's, but they have since moved away. We continue to do the best we can with what we've got in our little town and community. I used to think that the year 2020 was so far in the future and that it was almost Star-Trek like, but as we approach that year and as I look back over the past 20 years or so, I can honestly say that I've really enjoyed the journey to this point.

Chapter 5: The View from a Porch and Patio

When I first thought about this book, I had no idea how exhilarating and reflective the project and process would be. I have tried to capture the essence of my documented experiences here as candidly and frankly as possible. I have, in some cases, changed names and purposefully excluded others so that my treatment of others in my life story is both humane and appreciative. It was never my goal to embarrass anyone or put anybody out on "front street." With this in mind, let me conclude with some reflections and revelations.

As I sit on a very special porch, it is a late spring morning and the birds are singing. The sun is pleasantly caressing my skin and baldhead. I can hear a lawn mower off in the distance, a dog barking next door, and the voices of children across the street. In this peaceful moment, I feel compelled to reflect on the successful strategies and coping skills I have used throughout my career to find peace and settle myself.

The first of these is what I would call "signaling." It has both an internal and external component, but its purpose is to alert those around me of my coming, presence, and departure. I don't remember exactly when I started doing this, but those who know me best will tell you that there is rarely a time that I am not either whistling or humming as I go through my day. These are my signals and signatures. I use them as locators for myself and as a means of conveying to others both my internal and external disposition at that time. When I hum, it usually reflects an internal sense of happiness and contentment. My whistling is intended to convey to those around me that they too can be happy and content. In many ways, this is not unlike the countless ways that sighted persons communicate their disposition nonverbally to one another through a passing smile or head nod. This strategy was never more apparent to me than when I had my first experience of inviting a totally deaf faculty member to come into my differently abled class as a guest presenter. The experience became most memorable when the sign language interpreter was late for the presentation, preventing my deaf colleague from beginning their lecture. You can only imagine the communication challenges between a totally blind and totally deaf faculty member. At one point my colleague came up to me and warmly shook my hand to convey that he was there and ready to proceed, but could not because the interpreter was not present. He also wrote brief messages on the board to convey our dilemma to the class. At some point we stepped outside the classroom and, as we waited for the interpreter to arrive, we resorted to communicating with each other via text messaging. Imagine the significance of 21st Century technology within this context. We managed to sign and signal to each other as needed until the interpreter arrived—only 30 minutes late. I found out from my colleague that this was a common experience in his world. I thought to myself, "I can't imagine being that dependent on someone." In this case, my whistling or humming would have been ineffective to say the least. Over the years, I have found ways to use this signaling strategy to disarm those who might be uncomfortable with either my blindness or my blackness. Sprinkled with a nice dose of humor and carefully placed verbalizations, this disarming tactic has served me well most of the time.

Sensitive listening has been a critical part of my life as you might expect because it has allowed me to reach and convey a level of empathy that is often unattainable otherwise. I have had a number of experiences where I have literally been able to hear the pain and concern in someone's voice and it has allowed me to convey empathy and compassion. Often this listening strategy has allowed me to hear what is not said in addition to what is uttered – to more effectively read between the lines of someone's utterances. I think it is this strategy that has facilitated a class environment that has encouraged significant self-disclosure at times. I have had students share some amazing experiences in some of my classes that, quite frankly, at times, I did not know how to respond or how to address (ranging from stories of incest to suicidal attempts). I think it has happened so much because my students felt comfortable doing so, but I must admit it did usher in some discomfort and dissonance from time to time. As I sit on this porch, I am thinking about one class session from my differently abled class that I wish to this day I had tangibly captured in some way.

One of my previous students that had taken that class as a TAB was the guest speaker that day. When she took my class a few years earlier, she had been this statuesque woman that rode motorcycles and horses and loved fast cars. As a result of a very tragic car accident, she would be presenting in my class on this day for the first time as a permanent wheelchair user with paralysis from the neck down. I vividly remember her calling me from the hospital as she was recuperating and coming to terms with what the accident would mean for her daily life. Now here she was several years later addressing my class and, for the very first time, talking about the accident and the subsequent personal aftermath of it all. As you might expect, it was emotionally and physically gut wrenching. There were times when I felt guilty for inviting her to do it, but despite my repeated offers for her to stop she carried on and reassured me, "If I don't do it now, I may never talk about it. And I really need to." I am so happy to say that after that first presentation she would return to my class three or four more times to give a similar presentation. Each time sounding more confident and courageous than before. Every time she came to my class we all sat enraptured by her story but more importantly by her courage. I am honored that she felt comfortable sharing in that context. No, blind people cannot hear a pin drop two blocks away, but I do think that our dependence on listening can give some of us the capacity to reach a level of empathy that exceeds the normal expectations of others.

As I've gotten older, I've discovered the power and salience of silence. I used to make jokes about what is frequently referred to as the "silent treatment," but now I've learned that silence as a strategy and coping skill can be quite communicative. For a number of reasons, I decided to take a vow of silence in terms of verbally communicating in faculty meetings for about a year in 2010. It was both liberating and frustrating. I learned that several of my colleagues were troubled by my silence and both wanted and needed me to verbally contribute in such meetings. I also learned that my silence mostly went unobserved by many of my other colleagues. This strategy enabled me to really listen to others and convey a certain amount of fidelity to some of the issues under discussion that year. I remember how I felt hearing the sound of my own voice when I resumed speaking; it was deafening and almost eerie in some ways. That experience taught me the power and significance of silence in communicative interactions. Since issues of race and ethnicity and differently abled issues can often be controversial and complex, sometimes silence is the most effective way to communicate.

The final strategy that I think has served me over the years is what I will call "isolation." In 2016, two things occurred that I thought I would never see in my lifetime. The first was the election of Donald Trump as President of the United States and the second was the winning of the World Series by my beloved Chicago Cubs. I will not comment on President Trump here, but let it suffice to say that the Cubs winning the World Series was so incredible and so unexpected that I not only cried that night, but I felt a sense of exhilaration never before experienced. I literally wanted to resurrect some of my family members that had been long time Cubs fans so that we could share the moment together.

During that same academic year (2016-2017), something else happened that still lingers with me today. That year we had conducted yet another faculty search and this time one of the finalists we brought to campus happened to be a Black female. As I sat with her at dinner, it struck me just how lonely I was. I was not prepared for my physical and emotional response to her unsuccessful attempt to join our faculty. It struck me how isolating my world was in my department and how lonely I was, especially culturally. It took me several months to recover from what seemed like a teasing experience for me. I concluded that everybody needs somebody they can rely on and relate to on not just a human level, but a racial and cultural one as well. This is not an indictment of any of my present colleagues. This situation just conveyed to me how the role of isolation had not only crept into my academic existence, but probably allowed me to survive as long as I have. In some ways, I've always been a loner or "the only one." I was the only blind student to graduate in my high school class and the only blind student to graduate in my Bachelor's and Master's classes as well. So yes, I should have been used to it. That search experience, though, made me aware of just how desensitized I had become to my own isolation.

So I've left the porch now and I'm sitting on a patio, which causes me to think about the factors that I feel have made my story possible.

It starts with my faith. From the age of seven, when I became a Christian, my faith has sustained me. When I pray, I feel that I am praying to someone that's bigger than I. This relationship has been my constant friend and companion throughout my thirty years of academia. As I sit in this comfortable patio chair, I am happy for a supportive family—the one I have now and the one that was created by my grandparents as I was growing up. I am truly blessed to have had the unconditional love and support of family members down through the years. I can still remember my dependable Grandfather picking me up after a long day of classes and the wonderful meals that my Grandmother cooked to sustain me through the years, both physically and emotionally. I have been blessed with continuous physical health and emotional wellbeing. Until 2018, I had all 32 of my teeth and never had one cavity. I had two teeth extracted in 2018, but I'm doing alright. Finally, I have been blessed with the opportunity of freedom and liberty because of this wonderful country we live in. Recently, I sat beside a service member on a flight back to Columbus. Not only did I thank them for their service, but I gushed with pride at their conversation and commitment to our Armed Forces. What a country we live in. It has allowed a blind, Black boy from the South side of Chicago to grow up, make more good choices than bad ones, and have the experience of putting those down in a book like this. It might be helpful to revisit my title at this point of my story, especially the "back of the bus" aspect of it. I chose this part of the title because on the face of it there was a time when the back of the bus might have been a place of expectation for me, based on my blindness and blackness. Due to the sacrifice and commitment of others, I have had opportunities and experiences that have allowed me to be considered for every seat on the bus. However, I still believe in the minds and hearts of some others that, if they could make it happen, the back of the bus would probably still be the place they would choose for me, in many cases. The view from the front of the classroom, for me, is a view of control, acceptance, and trust.

I've thought long and hard about how to end this book and chapter. I thought the best way was to share some excerpts from one of my favorite poems. The poem is entitled "Painted on my Mind".

I can't see the sun, but I can feel its glow
I can't see a child, but I can hear them grow
I can't see a timepiece, but I can count the hours
I can't see a garden, but I can smell the flowers
I can't see a house, but I can feel a home
I can't see you standing there, but I know when I'm not alone
I may not be able to find a hillside
Or a rainbow, I'll never find
But believe me, I'm not missing out on life
Because it's painted on my mind

jw Smith Ph.D.

EDUCATION   **WAYNE STATE UNIVERSITY** Detroit, MI
Ph.D. - Speech Communication, May- 1989
Dissertation Topic: A Rhetorical Analysis of William Lucas in the 1986
    Gubernatorial Race in Michigan
Dissertation Advisor: Dr. Bernard L. Brock

PURDUE UNIVERSITY CALUMET Hammond, IN
Master of Arts - Speech Communication, May 1985

INDIANA UNIVERSITY NORTHWEST Gary, IN
Bachelor of Arts - History, May 1982

HONORS/APPOINTMENTS

2017-2018 Outstanding Graduate Mentor of the Year Award
2017-2018 Vice Chair of the newly formed State Rehabilitation Council (SRC) of OOD
(Opportunities for Ohioans with Disabilities) – Appointment by Ohio Governor
2007 NAACP Image Award for Research and Teaching
2004 National Federation of the Blind Educator of the Year Award
1999-2000 Chair of National Communication Assoc. Caucus on Disabilities
2000-2003 National Communication Assoc. Legislative Council
1999-2003 Board of Directors Local Chapter Red Cross International
1998-2001 Ohio Governor's Council on People with Disabilities
1998 Ohio University Teaching Colloquium
1997 Vice Chair of NCA Caucus on Disabilities
1995 Ohio University Asanti Award
1995 Central States Speech Communication Teaching Award
1992 Indiana University Faculty Colloquium on Excellence in Teaching Award

EMPLOYMENT HISTORY

OHIO UNIVERSITY, SCHOOL OF COMMUNICATION STUDIES
Athens, OH

6/99 – Present   *Associate Professor of Communication Studies*
Courses taught: COMS 780 Special Topics; COMS 740 Rhetorical Criticism;
COMS 643 Religious Rhetoric; COMS 450 Capstone, Race and Communication;
Tier III 435B/497R Black Communication Styles; COMS 430/530 Communica-
tion in Campaigns; COMS 411/511/469 Communicating with the Physically
Disabled; POCO 401, Political Communication; COMS 353, Contemporary
Rhetoric; COMS 352 Political Rhetoric; COMS 342, Communication and
Persuasion, COMS 250 History of Rhetorical Theory; COMS 220 Oral
Interpretation; COMS 206 Interpersonal Communication; COMS 110,
Communication between Cultures; COMS 103 Public Speaking.

7/13 – 7/14   *Interim Director of Honors Tutorial Studies*
Acted as academic adviser. Worked with school colleagues to arrange tutorials.
Conducted admissions
Interviews. Coordinated programs of study. For more information visit the HTC website.

8/12 – 5/13   *Interim Undergraduate Director*

Processed undergraduate admissions/transfers into the school. Communicated with prospective and new admits into the school. Met with and advised prospective students and their parents. Approved/enforced school policies and procedures. Addressed and processed student grievances. Assigned advisors. Submitted periodic updates to the faculty concerning 1) enrollment figures, 2) changes in policy and procedures, 3) advising reports.

6/99 – 6/02   *Undergraduate Director*
Processed undergraduate admissions/transfers into the school. Communicated with prospective and new admits into the school. Met with and advised prospective students and their parents. Approved/enforced school policies and procedures. Addressed and processed student grievances. Determined COMS Day undergraduate award winners. Assigned advisors. Submitted periodic updates to the faculty concerning 1) enrollment figures, 2) changes in policy and procedures, 3) students in academic peril, 4) advising reports.

9/93 – 6/99   *Assistant Professor of Speech Communication*
Courses taught: COMS 780 Special Topics; COMS 740 Rhetorical Criticism; COMS 700C Graduate Pro-Seminar; COMS 643 Religious Rhetoric; COMS 450 Race and Communication; Tier III 435B/497R Black Communication Styles; COMS 430/530 Communication in Campaigns; COMS 411/511/469 Communicating with the Physically Disabled; POCO 401 Political Communication; COMS 353 Contemporary Rhetoric; COMS 352 Political Rhetoric; COMS 342 Communication and Persuasion; COMS 303 Rhetorical Criticism; COMS 250 History of Rhetorical Theory; COMS 220 Oral Interpretation; COMS 206 Interpersonal Communication; COMS 110 Communication between Cultures; COMS 103 Public Speaking.

* Please note that as of May 2003, our school name changed from Interpersonal Communication (INCO) to Communication Studies (COMS)

1/89 - 8/93   **INDIANA UNIVERSITY SOUTH BEND** South Bend, IN
Assistant Professor of Speech Communication
Courses taught: S444 Political Communication; S426 Speech Making After 1945; S421 Rhetorical Criticism; S337 Rhetoric of Modern Dissent; S324 Persuasive Speaking; S323 Speech Composition; S322 Rhetoric and Modern Discourse; S321 History of Rhetorical Theory; S238 Communication in Black America; S223 Business and Professional Speaking; S221 Speech and Human Behavior; S130 Basic Speech for Honors; S121 Basic Fundamentals of Speech

Visiting Lecturer of Speech Communication
Courses taught: J410-Media As A Social Institution; S223 Business and Professional Speaking; S121 Basic Fundamentals of Speech;

1/88 - 12/88   **UNIVERSITY OF DETROIT** , MI
Faculty Part-Time
Course taught: SPC 100 Basic Speech Course

8/85 - 12/88   **WAYNE STATE UNIVERSITY** Detroit, MI
Faculty Part-time
Courses taught: Project 350 Basic Speech; SPB 215 Interpersonal Communication; SPC 215 Persuasion; SPB 0200, 101, 102 Basic Speech;

Graduate Assistant
Courses taught: SPB 0200, 101,102-Basic Speech; SPC 215 Persuasion; SPB 215-Interpersonal Communication

1/84 - 8/85	**PURDUE UNIVERSITY CALUMET** Hammond, IN *Graduate Assistant* Courses taught: SPC 114, 115 Basic Speech; SPC 224 Small Group Dynamic; Tutoring in other related areas *Faculty Part-time* Course taught: SPC 114 Basic Speech - Upward Bound
9/80 - 5/82	**INDIANA UNIVERSITY NORTHWEST** Gary, IN *Faculty Part-time* Course taught: S121 Basic Speech *Special Tutor* Tutored students in History, Geology, French
1/81 - 12/81	**LAKE COUNTY ASSOCIATION FOR THE MENTALLY RETARDED** Gary, IN *Music Therapist* Provided appropriate music and counseling for the mentally retarded

PROFESSIONAL ASSOCIATIONS
State Rehabilitation Council of Opportunities for Ohioans with Disabilities
National Communication Association
Central States Communication Association
National Federation of the Blind
National Federation of the Blind – Ohio (President 2008 – 2012)
Ohio Rehabilitation Services Commission Consumer Advisory Committee
National Association of Blind Educators
Ohio Governor's Council on People with Disabilities

UNIVERSITY SERVICE
OHIO UNIVERSITY Athens, OH
Department Level:
    Grievance Committee
    Curriculum Committee
    Goals Committee
    Graduate Committee
    Search and Screen Committee
    Alumni Relations Committee
    Assessment Committee
    Boase Prize Committee
    Awards Committee
    Promotion and Tenure Committee
    Directors Ad Hoc Committee
    Department Merit Committee
    Technology Committee
College Level:
    Professional Ethics Committee
    Scholarship
    Co-Chair of Diversity Task Force
    Senate Representative
    Dean's Advisory Council
University Level:
    President's Advisory Council on People with Disabilities
Ohio Fellows Faculty Mentor (2012-2015)

Program Description: The Ohio Fellows program is a non-traditional scholars' program that fosters in-depth learning, and engagement through close collaboration with visiting scholars, faculty, peers, and Ohio Fellows alumni.

Coordinating Council for Economic & Community Development

Scholarship

Admission and Recruiting

Advisor, College Republicans

Disabilities Advisory Committee

Enrollment Management Committee

General Education Outcomes Committee

Vision Ohio Implementation Committee

Disability Coordinator Search Committee

Vice President of Student Affairs Search Committee

INDIANA UNIVERSITY SOUTH BEND South Bend, IN

University Level:

Handicapped Student Association - Faculty Advisor

Affirmative Action Committee

Honors Advisory Board

Black Council

Academic Senate Parliamentarian

Senate Personnel Committee - Chairman

American Studies Committee

Faculty Welfare Committee

Chancellor's Review Committee

Division Level:

Speech and Rhetoric Club - Faculty Advisor

Curriculum Committee

Budget Committee

Community Level:

Hansel Neighborhood Center - Board of Directors

PAPERS

11/18   Sherwani, S. I., & Smith, J. W. (2018). Widening the dialogue and slimming the gap: Strong4Life childhood obesity health campaign. National Communication Association Conference, Salt Lake City, Utah.

04/18   Jenkins, E. M., & Smith, J.W. (2018, April). *'Your shirt looks great!' Young adults' preferred modalities and motivations for telling white lies to their peers.* Eastern Communication Association Conference, Pittsburgh, PA.

04/17   Razzante, R., & Smith, J.W. (2017, April). *Rhetorical re-framing and coutner narratives: An ideological critique of the Christian hip-hop artist Lecrae Moore.* Central State Speech Communication Association Conference, MN. (Karlyn Kohrs Campbell Award Recipient).

11/14   Smith, J.W. (2014, November). *Reclaiming our past: The significance of the African renaissance in the development of African American rhetorical theory.* National Communication Association Conference, Chicago, IL.

11/13   Smith, J.W. (2013, November). *(Dis)ability membership.* National Communication Association Conference, Washington, D.C.

04/13   Smith, J.W. (2013, April). *Conventions of defining success: GOP and DNC claims of success.* Midwest Political Science Association, Chicago, IL.

04/11   Smith, J.W. (2011, April). *In honor of Kenneth Jernigan: Argumentative functions of history in the 1990 banquet address to the National Federation of the Blind.* Central States Communication Association Conference Top Paper, Cleveland, OH.

11/06   Smith, J.W. (2006, November). *FDR and warm springs: Front stage, backstage.* National Communication Association Conference, Chicago, IL.

11/04   Smith, J.W. (2004, November). *Size and smirks: Viewing political debates without sight.* National Communication Association Conference, Chicago, IL.

11/04   Smith, J.W. (2004, November). *"Why do you wear those shades? Communicating competence in the classroom.* National Communication Association Conference, Chicago, IL.

11/04   Smith, J.W. (2004, November). *From the pit to the palace: A narrative paradigmatic pilgrimage of a Black preacher.* National Communication Association Conference, Chicago, IL.

11/01   Smith, J.W. (2001, November). *Myth or reality- Is there a blind culture?* National Communication Association Conference, Atlanta, GA.

11/97   Smith, J.W. (1997, November). *Disability concerns caucus: Expanding diversity and inclusion: Addressing the needs of the disabled culture in the university.* National Communication Association Conference, Chicago, IL.

11/97   Smith, J.W. (1997, November). *Experiential learning in communication commission: The role of teacher assessment in service-learning projects.* National Communication Association Conference, Chicago, IL.

11/97   Smith, J.W. (1997, November). *Political communication division: House Speaker Henry Clay's nationalism as unification- an extension of transcendent eloquence.* National Communication Association Conference, Chicago, IL.

11/96   Smith, J.W. (1996, November). *Instructors with disabilities in the classroom: Helping able bodied students overcome the handicap of stereotypes.* Speech Communication Association Convention, San Diego, CA.

11/95   Smith, J.W. (1995, November). *Philosophical and pedagogical concerns in implementing service learning in the traditional campaign course.* Speech Communication Association Convention, San Antonio, TX.

11/94   Smith, J.W. (1994, November). *Universal language of Black gospel music- A postmodern critique.* Speech Communication Association Convention, New Orleans, LA.

11/94   Smith, J.W. (1994, November). *A case study of the 1986 Michigan Gubernatorial campaign - Lessons and strategies for African American candidates seeking state and national offices.* Speech Communication Association Convention, New Orleans, LA.

11/93   Smith, J.W. (1993, November). *Cultural communication and Afrocentrism- Some rhetorical implications of a new world order.* Speech Communication Association Convention, Miami, FL.

4/93   Smith, J.W. (1993, April). *The contemporary message of Black gospel music- Social reality and rhetorical pragmatism.* Central States Speech Communication Association Convention, Lexington, KY.

4/92	Smith, J.W. (1992, April). *The rhetorical implication of African American children in literature.* Central States Speech Communication Association Convention, Cleveland, OH.
4/92	Smith, J.W. (1992, April). *Jim Baker and the PTL ministry- A Burkian perspective.* Central States Speech Communication Association Convention, Cleveland, OH.
4/91	Smith, J.W. (1991, April). *The effects of Oreo politics on Michigan's African American community.* Central States Speech Communication Association Convention, Chicago, IL.
4/91	Smith, J.W. (1991, April). *A case study of Jim Baker and the PTL ministry- Religion and the American dream.* Central States Speech Communication Association Convention, Chicago, IL.
11/90	Smith, J.W. (1990, November). *Jim Baker and the PTL ministry- A religious soap opera.* Speech Communication Association Convention, Chicago, IL.

PRESENTATIONS

03/16	Smith, J.W. (2016, March). Abilities conference presentation. Ohio University Southern Campus: Ironton, OH.
11/15	Smith, J.W. (2015, November). Communication and people with disabilities: Embracing opportunities – pedagogical and pragmatic methodologies. National Communication Association; NCA Convention, Las Vegas, NV.
10/13	Smith, J.W. (2013, October). Contemplating and confronting diversity and disability in the workplace. DisAbility Jobs Summit Presentation.
03/13	Smith, J.W. (2013, March). Don't forget about us—The non-visual perspective. Ohio University Conference: Tech Ability Presentation.

10/11   Smith, J.W. (2011, October). Four keys to effective communication between people with disabilities and those without. Featured Speaker at OU-Ironton, Disability Day.

09/11   Smith, J.W. (2011, September). Effective communication – The key to success. Keynote Speaker at Hocking College, SMART Week.

01/11   Smith, J.W. (2011, January). MLK Day Keynote Address-Rio Grande University; Ohio University Day of Diversity Panelist.

07/10   Smith, J.W. (2010, July). *Four keys to effective communication between persons with disabilities and temporarily able-bodied individuals (TABS).* National Association of Multicultural Rehabilitation Concerns Conference (NAMRC), Las Vegas, NV.

1/08   Smith, J.W. (2008, January). *MLK Day, keynote address.* Ohio University, Southern Campus.

12/07   Smith, J.W. (2007, December). *Four keys to effective communication between persons with disabilities and temporarily able-bodied individuals (TABS).* Ohio Prevention and Education Conference Workshop, Columbus, Ohio.

7/07   Smith, J.W. (2007, July). *Strategies for effective advocacy.* National Federation of the Blind Convention, Atlanta, GA.

3/07   Smith, J.W. (2007, March). *Four keys to effective communication between persons with disabilities and temporarily able-bodied individuals (TABS).* Vermont Department of the Blind and Visually Impaired- guest lecture series, Brattleboro VT and Keene, NH.

7/06   Smith, J.W. (2006, July). *Mentoring the young scholar.* NFB Convention, Dallas, TX.

11/05   Smith, J.W. (2005, November). Dialogue on Disability Panelist Participant, Ohio University, Athens, OH.

10/05	Smith, J.W. (2005, October). Pioneers in Education Presentation, Marietta College, Marietta, OH.
10/05	Smith, J.W. (2005, October). *Keynote address.* Music Therapist State Conference, Ohio University, Athens OH.
4/05	Smith, J.W. (2005, April). Disability Day Presentation, Ohio University, Athens, OH.
5/04	Smith, J.W. (2004, May). Panel Presentation Commemorating Malcom X, Ohio University, Athens, OH.
1/04	Smith, J.W. (2004, January). *Dr. Martin Luther King, keynote address.* Lake Forest College, Lake Forest, IL.
1/03	Smith, J.W. (2003, January). *Dr. Martin Luther King Day keynote address.* Marietta College, Marietta, OH.
1/02	Smith, J.W. (2002, January). *Dr. Martin Luther King Day keynote address.* Ohio University, Athens, OH.
1/00	Smith, J.W. (2000, January). *Dr. Martin Luther King, keynote address.* Lake Forest College, Lake Forest, IL.
6/98	Smith, J.W. (1998, June). *Reflecting the flame and passing the torch: Insuring the legacy, legitimacy and longevity of the NCA Black caucus- Keynote address.* National Communication Association Black Caucus, Baltimore, MD.
6/98	Smith, J.W. (1998, June). *Changing what it means to be blind- Keynote address.* Ohio State School for the Blind Bi-Annual Family Conference, Columbus, OH.
11/97	Smith, J.W. (1997, November). *Black caucus: Selective recall: Justice Thomas as a lawn jockey for the far right- panelist.* National Communication Association, Chicago, IL.
11/97	Smith, J.W. (1997, November). *Short course #17 Instructor- Communication with the physically disabled.* National Communication Association, Chicago, IL.

10/97	Smith, J.W. (1997, October). *Expanding the term disability- Keynote address*. Ohio Rehabilitation Association, Athens, OH.
10/97	Smith, J.W. (1997, October). *Music therapy: An effective rehab tool*. Ohio Rehabilitation Association, Athens, OH.
10/97	Smith, J.W. (1997, October). *Strategies for effective client/consumer communication*. Ohio Rehabilitation Association, Athens, OH.
1/97	Smith, J.W. (1997, January). *Martin Luther King, guest lecturer*. Ohio University, Chillicothe, OH.
12/96	Smith, J.W. (1996, December). *Service learning and the campaign, guest lecturer*. Ohio University, Athens, OH.
11/96	Smith, J.W. (1996, November). *African American narratives and narratological analysis, chair*. Speech Communication Association Convention, San Diego, CA.
11/96	Smith, J.W. (1996, November). *Taking the helm through service learning: Connecting communication curriculum with the community, chair*. Speech Communication Association Convention, San Diego, CA.
11/96	Smith, J.W. (1996, November). *Multiple perspectives, multiple approaches, multiple meanings: Inhaling the impact of waiting to exhale, respondent*. Speech Communication Association Convention, San Diego, CA.
10/96	Smith, J.W. (1996, October). *Arts and disabilities class- Guest lecturer*. Ohio University, Athens, OH.
10/96	Smith, J.W. (1996, October). *Communication with the physically disabled- Workshop guest lecturer*. Indiana University South Bend, South Bend, IN.
8/96	Smith, J.W. (1996, August). *Developing your presentation skills, guest lecturer*. Ohio University College of Medicine Minority Students, Athens, OH.
8/96	Smith, J.W. (1996, August). *Communicating with the physically disabled*. Ohio University College of Medicine- Eco Culture Course, Athens, OH.

8/96	Smith, J.W. (1996, August). *Communication with the physically disabled, guest lecturer.* Rehabilitation Counselors, Athens, OH.
7/96	Smith, J.W. (1996, July). *Developing your presentation skills- Guest lecturer.* Ohio University College of Medicine Minority Students, Athens, OH.
5/96	Smith, J.W. (1996, May). *Arts and disabilities class, guest lecturer.* Ohio University, Athens, OH.
5/96	Smith, J.W. (1996, May). *Communication with the physically disabled, guest lecturer.* Ohio University College of Medicine, Athens, OH.
3/96	Smith, J.W. (1996, March). *Athens Braille workshop- organizer and guest lecturer.* Bureau of Services for the Visually Impaired, Athens, OH.
2/96	Smith, J.W. (1996, February). *Arts and disabilities class- guest lecturer.* Ohio University, Athens, OH.
10/95	Smith, J.W. (1995, October). *Arts and disabilities class- guest lecturer.* Ohio University, Athens, OH.
6/95	Smith, J.W. (1995, June). *Tier III course development seminar panelist.* Ohio University, Athens, OH.
5/95	Smith, J.W. (1995, May). *Merits of education, guest lecturer.* Delta Gamma, Ohio University, Athens, OH.
5/95	Smith, J.W. (1995, May). *Arts and disabilities class, guest lecturer.* Ohio University, Athens, OH.
5/95	Smith, J.W. (1995, May). *Seminar, Convener.* National Federation of the Blind, Athens, OH.
3/95	Smith, J.W. (1995, March). *Arts and disabilities class, guest lecturer.* Ohio University, Athens, OH.
2/95	Smith, J.W. (1995, February). *Student activity board, guest lecturer.* Ohio University, Athens, OH.

2/95	Smith, J.W. (1995, February). *Black man think tank, guest lecturer.* Ohio University, Athens, OH.
10/94	Smith, J.W. (1994, October). *Merits of education, guest lecturer.* Delta Gamma, Ohio University, Athens, OH.
5/94	Smith, J.W. (1994, May). *Pre-Graduation ceremony, guest lecturer.* Purdue Calumet University, Hammond, IN.
5/94	Smith, J.W. (1994, May). *Disability awareness, panelist.* Ohio University Affirmative Action, Athens, OH.
5/94	Smith, J.W. (1994, May). *National Federation of the Blind colloquium, panelist and sponsor.* Ohio University, Athens, OH.
3/94	Smith, J.W. (1994, March). *Black man think tank, guest lecturer.* Ohio University, Athens, OH.
11/92	Smith, J.W. (1992, November). *On acting as a Burkian.* Speech Communication Association Convention, Chicago, IL.
10/92	Smith, J.W. (1992, October). *Economics and the 1992 Presidential campaign.* Indiana University South Bend Forum, South Bend, IN.
4/91	Smith, J.W. (1991, April). *The effects of Oreo politics on Michigan's African American community.* Indiana University South Bend Dean's Seminar, South Bend, IN.
3/90	Smith, J.W. (1990, March). *Creating a supportive work environment through effective communication.* Saint Joseph Hospital of Mishawaka Seminar, Mishawaka, IN.
2/90	Smith, J.W. (1990, February). *The do's and don'ts of parliamentary procedure.* Bethel Baptist Church Workshop, South Bend, IN.
10/89	Smith, J.W. (1989, October). *Interviewing as an effective screening tool.* Saint Joseph Hospital of Mishawaka Seminar, Mishawaka, IN.

PUBLICATIONS

2018   Razzante, R. & Smith, J.W. (2018). Rhetorical re-framing and counter narratives: An ideological critique of the Christian hip-hop artist Lecrae Moore. *Ohio Communication Journal, 56,* 59-68.

2017   Smith, J. W., Dohling, S., & Rush, K. (2017). Exploring communication between the differently abled and temporarily able-bodied in a special topics course. *In Pedagogy, disability and communication: Applying disability studies in the classroom.* Routledge: New York. (30-49).

2016   Smith, J. W. (2016). In their own words: The historical and rhetorical significance of the annual banquet address at the National Federation of the Blind convention. *Braille Monitor, 59*(1).

2015   Smith, J.W. (2015). *Communication and campaigns* (3rd ed.). Dubuque, IA: Kendall Hunt Publishing Company.

2014   Smith, J.W. (2014). Driving the affiliate: Some musings of a former affiliate President. *Braille Monitor 57*(6).

2009   Smith, J.W. (2009). *From pit to the palace. Strategies for discovering His purpose and your destiny.* Esperanza Communications.

2009   Smith, J.W. (2009). Four keys to effective communication between the able-bodied and people with disabilities. *Spectra,* 9-10.

2008   Quinlan, M., Smith, J. Webster, & Hayward, C. (2008). This car seems to be alive—Perspectives on the documentary *Plan F. Braille Monitor, 51*(4), 268-273.

2007   Smith, J.W. (2007). From the pit to the palace: A narrative paradigmatic pilgrimage of a black and blind preacher. *African American Pulpit.*

2007   Smith, J.W. (2007) *Essays on communication and the blind and visually impaired.* Columbus, OH: Zip Publishing.

2006   Smith, J.W. *"Why* do you wear those shades?" Communicating competence in the classroom. *Braille Monitor, 49*(3), 177-180.

2005	Smith, J.W. (2005). *Communication and campaigns* (2nd ed). Dubuque, IA: Kendall/Hunt Publishing Company.
2004	Smith, J.W. (2004). Pumping gas and reaching for the fans. *Braille Monitor*, *47*(7), 522-525.
2000	Smith, J.W. & Kandath, K.P. (2000). Communication and people who are visually impaired. In Braithwaite, D.O, & Thompson, T.L, *Handbook of Communication and People with Disabilities* (389-403). New York, NY: Routledge.
2000	Smith, J.W. & Colvert, A.L. (2000). What is reasonable. Workplace communication and people who are disabled. In Braithwaite, D.O. & Thompson, T. L. *Handbook of Communication and People with Disabilities* (131-158). New York, NY: Routledge.
1999	Smith, J.W. (1999). Forever climbing: An extraordinary Federationist still rises. *The Braille Monitor, 42*(2), 162-168.
1998	Smith, J.W. & Wood, A. F. (1998). *Communication and campaigns* (1st ed). Dubuque, IA: Kendall/Hunt Publishing Company.
1998	Smith, J. (1998). Culture, communication and Afrocentrism: Some rhetorical implications of a new world order. In Hamlet, J.D., *Afrocentric visions: Studies in culture and communication*, (107-118). Thousand Oaks, CA: SAGE Publishing.
1997	Smith, J.W. (1997). Disability simulation that works. *The Braille Monitor*, *(40)*4, 244-248.
1995	Smith, J.W. (1995). It's your move Son. *The Braille Monitor, 38*(7), 365-371.
1994	Smith, J.W. (1994). Race and reason - A black perspective on a dark issue. *The Braille Monitor, 37*(2), 112-114.
1993	Smith, J.W. (1993). Communicating care to the physically challenged. *Lake Union Herald*, 10-11.
1993	Smith, J.W. (1993). The American way: The evolution of a Federationist. *The Braille Monitor, 36*(6), 759-762.

1993   Smith, J.W. (1993). Assessing King's dream. *South Bend Tribune: Michi-*

ana Point of View, A9.

Appendix B – Sample Syllabus

COMS 8390: TOPICS IN THE PHILOSOPHY OF COMMUNICATION – RHETORIC AND PUBLIC CULTURE

Topic: Black Rhetoric

Instructor: Dr. jw Smith

Required Texts

Gilyard, K., & Banks, A. (2018). *On African-American rhetoric*. New York: Routledge.

Jackson, R. L. & Richardson, E. B. (2003). *Understanding African American rhetoric: Classical origins to contemporary innovations*. New York: Routledge. **(PDF Provided)**

Jackson, R. L. & Richardson, E. B. (2007). *African American rhetoric(s): Interdisciplinary perspectives*. Southern Illinois University Press.

Alim, H. S. & Smitherman, G. (2012). *Articulate while Black: Barack Obama, language, and race in the U. S.* Oxford University Press.

*In most cases, if not all, I will provide PDFs for you, but you should certainly feel free to purchase any of the readings on your own if you'd like. Additionally, understand that from time to time we will add readings as the class evolves.

Course Overview and Objectives

For a number of years, I taught a version of this class at the undergraduate level and I entitled it Black Styles of Communication. That course focused on significant Black orators and their roles in the historical and cultural development in our society. Additionally, we examined the role of the Black church, the influence of slavery, the impact of sports and entertainment and hip-hop culture within that same context. The class was then known as a Tier III class which was designed to be a synthesized capstone class for graduating seniors. I enjoyed teaching that class, but I always wanted to offer much of its content as well as additional material at the graduate level.

Our focus for this course will be more theoretical in nature and more topical versus chronological. To this end, our main objectives include 1) Examining relevant literature and research that has contributed to and continues to inform our understanding of the rhetorical, methodological, and pedagogical exigencies involved in the study of Black Rhetoric. Please note that I am purposefully using the term Black for a number of reasons and I am in strong agreement with Cummings and Daniel who "recognize that 'African American' is the preferred term to 'black';

however, to use the latter term is to deny other people of African descent their role in this communication phenomena. Therefore, both terms will be used." 2) To examine those principles, nuances, and historical/cultural developments that have helped to create and maintain the "Black style of communication", 3) To expand our knowledge of and appreciation for this unique area of research and to perhaps make future recommendations for study in this area.

Dialogic Learning Environment

I have provided the initial organizing framework of literature and course objectives. But you also need to figure out what <u>you</u> need/want to learn in this course. I firmly believe in the importance of what many scholars call "connected knowing." Connected knowing involves participants in the co-production of knowledge. I believe classrooms ought to be places that respect the narratives of participants as well as the narratives of disciplinary knowledge. One of my goals is to allow participants to explore their professional selves – explorations that can ultimately lead to connections between self and subject matter. We need to work together in order to enact this culture. Your cooperation and willingness to share your experiences and insights are essential. When a reading assignment is made, you are expected to come to class not only having read the material but prepared to discuss it in a meaningful way. My suggestion is that you take detailed notes while reading course materials. Bring your notes to class with you and be ready to discern primary contentions of readings, articulate defensible contentions and arguments of your own, ask well formulated questions, critique material, share insights and experiences, "play" with ideas, and risk transforming or enlarging your standpoint based on class dialogue. I don't expect that you will agree with everything you read. I certainly don't. However, even in disagreement, I've found our thinking stimulated to ask if there are other and perhaps more satisfying ways of communicating than those posited by our dominant disciplinary models and everyday practices and patterns. I will come to class ready to share my experiences, engage and challenge your analysis, reading, and writing skills. In sum, demonstrate intellectual curiosity, engage in classroom discussion, allow space for everyone's contribution, and encounter materials in ways that draw you out of and beyond yourself to potentially new ways of knowing and being in the world.

Course Policies

<u>Special needs</u>: If you have special needs or you have a disability which may affect your participation in the class, please see me as soon as possible so that I may accommodate your needs.

<u>Academic dishonesty</u>: Academic dishonesty of all sorts including plagiarism is a violation of Ohio University's academic policy and can result in course failure at the discretion of the instructor.

<u>Attendance/late work</u>: Your attendance is expected. A lot of what you will learn in this course will come from sharing ideas and listening to your peers share ideas. As a result, your attendance is strongly encouraged and expected.

Grading and Requirements

Assignments will be graded using a percentage system. The point breakdown below represents the maximum credit awarded for the primary assignment in this course: A seminar paper.

Assignment	Course Evaluation
Seminar Paper	70%
Reflection Paper	20%
Attendance and Participation	10%
Total	100%

Grade	Points
A	90-100%
B	80-89%
C	70-79%
D	60-69%
F	Under 60%

Reflection Paper

I believe that reflection and contemplation can be a valuable aspect of the learning process, especially given the complex nature of some of the content material in this course. With this in mind, I would like for you to engage in this process by submitting a 4- to 6-page reflection/reaction paper, excluding bibliographic and other ancillary materials.

Because we will be covering a great deal of information each week, you will be given broad latitude in the selection/focus of your reflections/reactions. Your selection might include classroom presentations, a piece of literature not covered in course materials, a particularly provocative media depiction, and/or a live presentation outside of our class experience that highlights or emphasizes significant relevant aspects of course content. This paper will allow you to explore in more detail some issue/aspect raised by a specific guest lecturer or other presentation in the class. In any case, your paper should be guided by some theoretical or conceptual ideas covered in course readings and discussions. Finally, your paper should suggest potential areas for future research in a particular area of our field, or should shine the spotlight on an underappreciated or underdeveloped area in our field. Your paper should conform to the latest version of the APA manual, and should contain a title page and abstract. Another purpose for this assignment is to allow me to see how you write and think and how I might be helpful to you in these areas.

Seminar Paper

One of your primary goals in this course should be to author a seminar paper exploring one of your interests in relation to (but not limited to) course materials. *Your seminar paper should demonstrate your ability to advance a knowledge claim that enriches disciplinary conversations and offers new possibilities for communication practices.* You may choose to continue working on a project that you started in another semester as long as the project relates to the nature of this seminar and significant progress on the project occurs through the course of this semester (e.g., you could collect and analyze discourse for a proposal that you wrote last semester). Alternatively, you could write a research proposal (modeled after the articles read in class) and include a problem statement/rationale and a synthesis and critique of literature from a particular theoretical standpoint (culminating in a set of research questions). In proposing a rhetorical analysis, you could include a problem statement/rationale, theoretical orientation, and preliminary discussion of artifacts and how you would analyze them. Irrespective of your epistemological position and method, you must demonstrate the ability to theoretically frame a problem/issue—systematically identify, analyze, and synthesize scholarly ideas as well as creatively propose new contributions to our disciplinary knowledge. With feedback, you should be able to continue deepening your arguments, in some cases collecting and analyzing discourse, and submit the manuscript to a conference and/or for potential publication. Like the readings you will encounter in this course, I want to be able to see how you are making connections between philosophies of communication covered in previous courses, contemporary applications of those theoretical positions, and the set of issues/concerns central to your knowledge claims. I am also open to alternative assignments that better allow you to reach your professional goals (e.g., working on a grant proposal or even a potential dissertation proposal and or chapter).

Tentative Schedule/Organization of Readings

Unit 1: Classical Egyptian Origins of African American Rhetoric

Week 1:

*PDFs provided for last three readings this week

Gilyard, K., & Banks, A. (2018). Historical overview of African-American rhetoric. In *On African-American Rhetoric*. p. 10-28.

Cummings, M. S. & Daniel, J. L. *The study of African American Rhetoric.*

103

Hamlet, J. D. (1998). Understanding African American Oratory: Manifestations of Nommo. In J. D. Hamlet's (Ed.) *Afrocentric Visions*. Pp. 89- 105.

Smith, J. W. (1998). Culture, communication, and Afrocentrism: Some rhetorical implications of a new world order. In J. D. Hamlet's (Ed.) *Afrocentric Visions*. Pp. 107- 117.

Week 2:

Gilyard, K., & Banks, A. (2018). Jeremiads and manifestoes. In *On African-American Rhetoric*. p. 29-45.

Karenga, M. (2003). Nommo, Kawaida, and communicative practice: Bringing good into the world. In Jackson & Richardson (Eds.) *Understanding African American rhetoric*. Pp. 3-22.

Alkebulan, A. A. (2003) The spiritual essence of African American rhetoric. In Jackson & Richardson (Eds.) *Understanding African American rhetoric*. Pp. 23-42.

Salazar, P. J. (2008). Rhetoric in Africa: Three encounters. *Nawa Journal of Language and Communication*, 2(2), 58-70.

Unit 2: Manifestations of African American Rhetoric and Orality

Week 3:

PDFs provided for last two readings this week

Cummings, M. S. & Latta, J. M. (2003). "Jesus is a rock": Spirituals and lived experience. In Jackson & Richardson (Eds.) *Understanding African American rhetoric*. Pp. 57-68.

Hamlet, J. D. The reason why we sing.

Pastor and Flock

Week 4:

Gilyard, K., & Banks, A. (2018). Rhetorical theory. In *On African-American Rhetoric*. p. 47-70.

Walker, F. R. & Greene, D. M. (2006). Exploring Afrocentricity: An analysis of the discourse of Jesse Jackson. *Journal of African American Studies*, 9(4), 61-71.

Spirituality, Identity, and the Rhetoric of Marcus Garvey. *PDF provided for this reading*

Unit 3: Politics of Defining African American Rhetoric

Week 5:

Royse, Pamela. (2011). Ideology, Space, and the Problem of Justice: The Lynching of Emmett Till. (Dissertation). *PDF provided*

McPhail, M. L. (2003). The politics of (in)visibility in African American rhetorical scholarship: A (re)quest for an African worldview. In Jackson & Richardson (Eds.) *Understanding African American rhetoric.* Pp. 99-114.

Jackson, R. L. (2003). Afrocentricity as metatheory: A dialogic exploration of its principles. In Jackson & Richardson (Eds.) *Understanding African American rhetoric.* Pp. 115-132.

Bates, B. R., Lawrence, W. Y. & Cervenka, M. (2008). Redrawing Afrocentrism: Visual *Nommo*, in George H. Ben Johnson's editorial cartoons. *The Howard Journal of Communications, 19,* 277-296.

Week 6:

Gorsevski, E. W. & Butterworth, M. L. (2011). Muhammad Ali's fighting words: The paradox of violence in nonviolent rhetoric. *Quarterly Journal of Speech, 97,* 50-73.

Griffin, R. A. (2012). I AM an angry Black woman: Black feminist autoethnography, voice, and resistance. *Women's Studies in Communication, 35,* 138-157.

Week 7:

Pause and reflect: Reflection papers due February 26th and 28th.

Unit 4: African American Rhetorical Analysis of Struggle and Resistance

Week 8:

Forbes, E. (2003). Every man fights for his freedom: The rhetoric of African American resistance in the mid-nineteenth century. In Jackson & Richardson (Eds.) *Understanding African American rhetoric.* Pp. 155-170.

Morrison, C. D. (2003) Death narratives from the killing fields: Narrative ciricism and the case of Tupc Shakur. In Jackson & Richardson (Eds.) *Understanding African American rhetoric.* Pp. 187-208.

Selby, G. S. (2002). Mocking the sacred: Frederick Douglass's 'Slaveholder Sermon' and the antebellum debate over religion and slavery. *Quarterly Journal of Speech, 88,* 326-341.

Terrill, R. E. (2003). Irony, silence, and time: Frederick Douglass on the fifth of July. *Quarterly Journal of Speech, 89,* 216-234.

Week 9:

Gaipa, M. (2007). "A creative psalm of brotherhood": The (de)constructive play in Martin Luther King's "Letter from Birmingham Jail." *Quarterly Journal of Speech, 93,* 279-307.

Owens, K. (2007). Myth making as a human communication paradigm: The case of Martin Luther King Jr., and the civil rights movement. *American Communication Journal, 9*(3).

McPhail, M. L. (1998). Passionate intensity: Louis Farrakhan and the fallacies of racial reasoning. *Quarterly Journal of Speech, 84*, 416-429.

Terrill, R. E. (2000). Colonizing the borderlands: Shifting circumference in the rhetoric of Malcom X. *Quarterly Journal of Speech, 86*, 67-85.

Unit 5: Trends and Innovations in Analyzing Contemporary African American Rhetoric

Week 10:

Dangerfield, C. L. (2003). Lauryn Hill as lyricist and womanist. In Jackson & Richardson (Eds.) *Understanding African American rhetoric.* Pp. 209-222.

Brown-White, S. (2003). Afrocentric rhetoric transcending audiences and contexts: A case study of preacher and politician Emanuel Cleaver II. . In Jackson & Richardson (Eds.) *Understanding African American rhetoric.* Pp. 263-284.

Gilyard, K., & Banks, A. (2018). Technology and African-American rhetoric. In *On African-American Rhetoric.* p. 71-73.

Gilyard, K., & Banks, A. (2018). Rhetoric and Black Twitter. In *On African-American Rhetoric.* p. 84-103.

Week 11:

Quinlan, M., Bates, B. R. & Webb, J. B. (2012). Michelle Obama 'got back': (Re)defining (counter)stereotypes Black Females. *Women and Language, 35*, 119-126.

Medhurst, M. J. (2010). George W. Bush as Goree Island: American slavery and the rhetoric of redemption. *Quarterly Journal of Speech, 96*, 257-277.

Hopson, M. C. (2003). Black feminist theorizing in bell hooks' "Happy to be Nappy." *PDF provided*

Moon, D. G. & Holling, M. A. (2017). *Race(ing) Intercultural Communication: Racial Logics in a Colorblind Era.* Routledge. *(Selected chapters – PDF provided)*

Week 12:

Black Rhetoric and the Obama Presidency

Alim, H. S. & Smitherman, G. (2012). *Articulate while Black: Barak Obama, language, and race in the U. S.* Oxford University Press.

Patia, K. G. (2017). Double-consciousness and the rhetoric of Barack Obama: The price and promise of citizenship. *Quarterly Journal of Speech, 103*(4), 426-431.

Unit 6: Visions for Research in African American Rhetoric

Week 13:

Asante, M. K. (2003). The future of African American rhetoric. . In Jackson & Richardson (Eds.) *Understanding African American rhetoric.* Pp. 285-292.

Pennington, D. L. (2003). The discourse of African American women. . In Jackson & Richardson (Eds.) *Understanding African American rhetoric.* Pp. 309-314.

Week 14:

Final paper presentations and discussions

About the Author

J. Webster Smith (J.W.), PhD was born blind on March 9, 1959 in Chicago, Illinois. He is the second of five children and most of his family yet resides in the Chicago area. His hobbies include reading, watching sports, singing and playing the piano/keyboards. Dr. Smith and his wife, Regina, have two daughters, Ebony and Joshelyn.

Dr. Smith attended the public schools in the Chicago and Northwest Indiana areas and graduated from Lew Wallace High School in Gary, Indiana in 1976. He received his Bachelor of Arts degree in History and Speech Communication from Indiana University in 1982, his Master of Arts degree in Speech Communication from Purdue University in 1985, and his PhD from Wayne State University in Detroit in 1989.

J.W. has worked as a music therapist and as a radio announcer, however since 1983, Dr. Smith has taught a variety of courses at the university level. Presently, Dr. Smith is a professor of Speech Communication in the School of Communication Studies at Ohio University in Athens, Ohio. Before this tenure, Dr. Smith served as professor of Speech Communication at Indiana University, South Bend.

Dr. Smith feels that as a blind African American it is essential that we expand the term 'diversity' and incorporate every effort necessary to create an environment that encourages openness and understanding. Dr. Smith often refers to non-disabled individuals as TABs, temporarily able-bodied individuals. He firmly believes that our differences can be our strengths and that many people live more for affirmation than bread and that we are each responsible to all for all.

Dr. Smith is a member of the National Communication Association, Central States Communication Association, National Federation of the Blind, National Federation of the Blind of Ohio, and the National Association of Blind Educators. In addition, Dr. Smith has served as a member of the Ohio State Library Consumer Advisory Committee and has served on the State Consumer Advisory Committee of the Ohio Rehabilitation Services Commission. Dr. Smith has also served on the Ohio Governor's Council on People with Disabilities. Dr. Smith served as President of the National Federation of the Blind of Ohio from 2008-2012. In 2018, Dr. Smith was selected by Governor John Kasich for a three-year term on the first State Rehabilitation Council (SRC) for Opportunities for Ohioans with Disabilities.

CPSIA information can be obtained
at www.ICGtesting.com
Printed in the USA
FSHW010845300120
66428FS

9 780578 579672